AF607905

Relational Sociology and Research on Schools, Colleges, and Universities

Relational Sociology and Research on Schools, Colleges, and Universities

Edited by

William G. Tierney and Suneal Kolluri

Published by State University of New York Press, Albany

Printed in the United States of America

For information, contact State University of New York Press, Albany, NY
www.sunypress.edu

Library of Congress Cataloging-in-Publication Data

Names: Tierney, William G., editor. | Kolluri, Suneal, editor.
Title: Relational sociology and research on schools, colleges, and universities / [edited by] William G. Tierney and Suneal Kolluri.
Description: Albany : State University of New York Press, 2020. | Includes bibliographical references and index.
Identifiers: LCCN 2019028973 | ISBN 9781438478234 (hardcover : alk. paper) | ISBN 9781438478258 (ebook)
Subjects: LCSH: Universities and colleges—United States—Sociological aspects. | Universities and colleges—Research—United States. | Educational sociology—United States.
Classification: LCC LC191.94 .R45 2020 | DDC 378.73—dc23
LC record available at https://lccn.loc.gov/2019028973

10 9 8 7 6 5 4 3 2 1

Contents

Illustrations and Tables

Figures

Tables

Acknowledgments

We thank Diane Flores, Monica Raad, and the rest of the team in the Pullias Center of Higher Education who supported the creation of this book. We also acknowledge Rebecca Colesworthy and our collaborators at SUNY Press for their careful stewardship of this publication. We know this book comes at a difficult time in the United States, and we hope this is a useful contribution to creating a more equitable world.

Introduction

Education, Equity, and the Promise of Seeing Relationally

SUNEAL KOLLURI AND WILLIAM G. TIERNEY

Seemingly unending streams of books, news articles, and academic journals have sought solutions to persistent challenges of educational inequity, yet educational stratifications continue to harden. Over the past few decades, achievement inequities by class (Reardon 2011) and gaps in access to selective postsecondary institutions by race and ethnicity (Posselt, Jaquette, Bielby, & Bastedo 2012) have widened. We make no claims to solving this puzzle, which has vexed decades of educational scholars. Educational inequity will persist long after this volume is published. We borrow from pragmatist sociological philosophy to offer new ways to analyze challenges in schools and colleges. For researchers digging for answers to entrenched problems in education, new tools can unearth insights that have remained stubbornly beyond their grasp. We suggest that relational sociology is an important theoretical and methodological innovation with wide-ranging applications to educational scholarship.

The mechanisms of educational stratification are only partially understood. For example, consider the persistent challenge of postsecondary education by race and class. The value of a good education is undisputed. Achievements like a high school diploma and a four-year degree provide increased access to well-paid jobs, insulation from economic downturns, improved health, and enhanced social connectedness (Bloom, Hartley, & Rososvsky 2007). However, many students, often from marginalized communities, forgo the pursuit of these credentials. Rates of high school graduation and bachelor's degree attainment among Black, Latinx, and low-income students are troubling. The US Census Bureau (2015) reports that among the US population between the ages of twenty-five and thirty-four, 32.8 percent of White people have attained a bachelor's degree, while only 22.5 percent of Black and 15.5 percent of Latinx people have attained one.

Researchers have adopted two primary ways of understanding these inequities (Perna 2006). First, they look to economic theories of individual choice and cost-benefit analyses of educational attainment. In these models, rational actors make educational decisions based on available information. Students who do not maximize individual gains from educational attainment likely presume themselves underprepared for subsequent academic pathways or are uninformed about future educational possibilities. Important research has uncovered the value of academic skill development (Adelman 2006) and enhanced information to students and parents (Dynarski, Libassi, Michelmore, & Owen 2018) to improving educational attainment outcomes.

Alternatively, sociologically inclined educational researchers argue that structural processes warrant more attention than does individual choice in understanding educational attainment gaps. Racial and socioeconomic oppressions constrain the choices available to marginalized students. Instead of seeing education inequities unfolding by way of individual decision making, schools are directly implicated in social reproduction. Bourdieu's (1986) influential theory of cultural capital suggests that schools reward the types of knowledge and dispositions cultivated in middle-class homes. High schools might tailor postsecondary opportunities to the class backgrounds of their students (McDonough 1998). Indeed, measures of cultural capital are closely associated with college degree attainment (DiMaggio & Mohr 1985). Critical race theorists such as Derrick Bell (1991) and Gloria Ladson-Billings (1995) argue that teachers and administrators use racist ideologies in schools that limit the educational opportunities of students of color. In particular, the theory of intersectionality has provided a useful lens for understanding how multiple identities along the lines of race, class, and gender affect social outcomes (Collins 2004; Crenshaw 1989). A robust line of scholarship has provided empirical support for the notion that schooling practices produce socioeconomic and racialized stratifications of educational attainment (Lewis 2003: Oakes 1985; Tyson 2011).

Rather than take sides in the debate over social structure or individual decision making, some have suggested that scholars investigate both

(Perna 2006). They reason that neither model is sufficient, and combining the frameworks allows for a fuller picture of inequities in college access. Information, choice, and prior preparation fail to explain all of the variance in educational attainment (Perna 2000). Approaches that assume the preeminence of structural oppressions, meanwhile, fail to explain the unique individual and cultural adaptations that allow some people from repressed groups to overcome their marginalization. Thus, Perna (2006) offers a conceptual model that understands college access by way of individual choices, economic contexts, school offerings, and student access to social and cultural capital. The solution to the inadequacies of college readiness research, therefore, is a "kitchen sink" approach, throwing an abundance of available theoretical constructs at a social problem to see its related social processes.

Relational sociologists attempt not to see more, but to see differently. They critique individualist and structural analyses for an overemphasis on essentialist attributes of individuals and institutions. The economic theories discussed above see individuals as static and atomistic. Structural theories grounded in critical and social reproduction theories see categorical groups—defined by class, gender, sexuality or other identities—as predetermined by inherent characteristics. Instead of looking first to categorical attributes, relational sociologists look to relationships. Individuals and groups certainly matter, but in a "bonds over essences" relational framework, social ties are given primacy. From a relational standpoint, equity-oriented researchers of college access might look beyond structural oppressions and individual attributes, instead investigating the dynamic social networks across primary, secondary, and postsecondary contexts that reify or undermine college-going inequities. As opposed to seeing the social world as defined by indelible traits of people or institutions, relational sociology looks to processes shaped by interactions among differently positioned actors whose realities are continually in flux. Thus, the social world is fiercely contested and frequently renegotiated among interconnected entities. The anti-essentialist approach, we suggest, can interrogate persistent challenges of educational inequity in ways that illuminate new avenues for sustained social change.

Anti-Essentialism and Educational Research

The critique we offer here centers on the matter of essentialism. In essentialist analyses, people and institutions are disconnected from one another and are mere vessels for their prescribed attributes. They have little power to shape their own realities. Relational sociology has at its core an "anti-categorical imperative" (Emirbayer 1996; Emirbayer & Goodwin 1994). Relational sociologists highlight network configurations rather than categorical attributes as the principal drivers of social processes. Theoretically, essentialism is a foil for relational sociology.

Relational sociology certainly does not eliminate the importance of categories of identity. Race/ethnicity, class, gender, sexuality, and other identities matter. Important work in sociology has articulated how these identities are defined by way of historical processes and dominant ideologies to shape opportunity structures for marginalized groups. What relational sociology adds is a more bottom-up framing of social reality. Social identities matter, but how they matter depends significantly on the shapes of the relational networks in which people are embedded—the social transactions they complete, the coalitions they assemble, and the power-laden fields of practice they engage. Identities are constructed not by way of inherent attributes or widely agreed-on "typifications" (Berger & Luckmann 1989), but in vigorous and multidirectional relational transactions within a social network. How one comes to understand the social meanings of identity markers like race and class occurs within bundles of social ties. Thus, identity matters, but it is not the starting point for a relational study. Rather, researchers must see social reality as the engagement of differently positioned actors in a social space whose transactions compel messy and uncertain educational processes. These dynamic engagements can reify or destabilize power dynamics and enhance or lessen the salience of established identity markers.

Rational actor models have been vigorously contested on the grounds that they neglect structural oppressions (Bourdieu & Wacquant 1992; Teranishi & Briscoe 2008). Structural racism and economic inequities constrain the potential of people to behave in ways that maximize their utility. However, structural analyses are also hamstrung by essentialism. They often imply that people are not actors but are acted on by formalized processes aligned with their personal attributes, such as race and class.

In conversations on unequal educational attainment by race and class, essentialist analyses prevail. Class and racial backgrounds weigh on student aspirations and determine the college preparatory opportunities of their high schools. If individuals have agency, that agency is viewed in terms of rational decision making based on available information about postsecondary options. A relational approach first sees how differently positioned actors within and outside of schools interact in processes related to educational attainment. These relational units are at the center of analyses and are presumed to be the drivers of social reality.

The central goal of this book is to help us rethink (and presumably redirect) educational conversations away from essentialist analyses. We offer relational sociology as a means by which to apply a new lens for viewing persistent challenges in the field of education. In what follows, we discuss the role of relationships in sociology, how "seeing relationally" reframes relationships to uncover a deeper understanding of educational processes, and how one might apply the tenets of relational sociology to the theory and practice of education.

Sociology and Relationships

Sociology is often defined in textbooks and course syllabi as the study of relationships. Thus the existence of a theory of relational sociology may seem redundant. What need is there for a discipline already about relationships to be revised to be more relational? In part, this book asserts the need for a better articulated vision for how relationships shape social life, a vision that has yet to be developed in educational scholarship.

Prominent theories of education have framed relationships in ways that actually disconnect people from one another as opposed to seeing them as they are—in continual processes of transactions with other social actors. Some sociologists elevate relationships by arguing that people's social realities are related to the class contexts in which they are raised. Family background is thus a barrier that inevitably obstructs the forward progress of working-class youth. These youth lack intergenerational closure (Coleman 1987); they are exposed to fewer words (Hart & Risley 1995); or they are isolated in neighborhoods that compel maladaptive behaviors (Anderson 2000). Alternatively, critical theorists view people as inescapably intertwined with pervasive and all-consuming social structures. By their account, student hardships are related to their oppressed position in established social hierarchies. Our suggestion here is that relationships in sociology are defined in essentialist terms more often than not. People are locked into all-encompassing relationships with their background characteristics or oppressive social systems. Rarely are people's relationships with other people viewed as the core driver of their social realities. Relational sociology's conception of relationships seeks to redress this theoretical oversight.

As we suggest in chapter 1, relational sociologists see one's relational reality as more dynamic—less of an inexorable march toward predictable social outcomes and more of an uncertain stagger along contested terrain. Relational sociologists highlight relationships as embedded in sociohistorical and spatiotemporal contexts. These contexts shape the nature of the relationship and the social processes that unfold for the related parties. In particular, borrowing from Bourdieu's field theory, relational theorists understand people as differently positioned in social arenas rife with conflict over scarce resources. These processes are informed by social contexts related to class and race but are predominantly framed by the nature of interpersonal interactions within the field. Thus, relational sociology does more than assert that relationships matter. Rather, relationships are at the core of social reality and are connected to a larger structure of hierarchies and systems that define a social sphere.

Seeing Relationally

The goal of this book is not to posit the supremacy of relational approaches over all others. We argue that a relational lens has the potential to help us make insightful contributions to educational theory. We focus on two ways that this might occur. First, relational sociology compels innovative methodologies that uncover the intricate connectedness of individuals in social worlds. Second, the emphasis on relational processes may uncover how inequity unfolds in educational settings.

A relational approach necessitates lenses on relationship structures, interpersonal transactions, and positions in the field. Such a multifaceted theoretical grounding necessitates scholarly approaches capable of capturing complex relational realities. In chapter 2, Joseph Ferrare puts forth a theoretical and methodological framework capable of rendering a relational view of the social world. For Ferrare, seeing relationally necessitates theoretical and methodological pluralism that borrows from sociological tools like social network analysis and sociological concepts such as field theory to understand educational processes. Because social processes unfold amidst bundles of relationships in and out of schools, social network analysis and field theory provide useful direction for educational researchers.

In chapter 3, Julie Posselt demonstrates how relationally analyzed data can tease out local power dynamics and suggest strategies for enhancing equitable access to higher education. She looks specifically at transcribed conversations among admissions officers at a prestigious university from constructivist, critical, and relational lenses. While each lens offers important insights, the relational lens merges structural and contextual analyses of data to elucidate how power is negotiated in situ. Seeing relationally can situate researchers amid the unfolding processes that direct social outcomes.

Researchers of race might also consider a relational approach. Race has often been seen as an essential category, and scholars of race often emphasize the inequitable characteristics of educational institutions as uniformly affecting racially minoritized youth. Thus, race scholarship often succumbs to structural essentialisms that suggest the inevitability of oppressive learning experiences. In a theoretical exploration of racial processes on college campuses, Antar Tichavakunda (chapter 4) asserts that relational sociology might allow for an understanding of race as shaped by a diverse cross-section of actors that coconstruct racial campus climates. Tichavakunda suggests that relational inquiries can problematize predominant framings of campus diversity and microaggressions. Seeing relationally may allow scholars to more holistically understand racial processes as they occur amid transactions between differently positioned actors on school campuses.

Relational Theory and Practice in Education

The foundations of this book are grounded in theory, which allows the advancement of scholarly knowledge by compounding the collective insights of centuries of researchers toward a deeper understanding of the social world. Kezar (2006) calls theories the "received wisdom" of earlier intellectuals. Theories can inspire particular sociological investigations (Burawoy 1998) as well as frame how research projects are designed and data are analyzed (Suppes 1974).

On one hand, theory is essential to educational research. On the other hand, education is a discipline with distinctly practical applications. However, approaches that elevate practical concerns devoid of theoretical considerations have the potential to produce ineffectual solutions to pressing challenges. For example, when educational research uncovered that digital inequities allowed some students more robust opportunities for online learning than others, superintendents across the nation implemented multimillion-dollar "one-to-one" technology policies that assigned every student a personal computing device. The logic informing these decisions is reasonable. Working-class families lack the financial resources to provide their children with technology that facilitates learning. Providing that technology is a practical approach to closing the digital divide. However, many of these policies have failed to meaningfully affect achievement gaps. Neglecting prominent theories of social reproduction leads to policies like one-to-one digital devices that overlook persistent drivers of inequity that may be immune to adjusted resource allocations (Tierney & Kolluri 2018).

Thus, we highlight the centrality of theory to social understanding, and we aim to keep a foothold in the practical realities of educational institutions. In particular, the empirical work in the book suggests how the theory of relational sociology can be used to better conceptualize student learning experiences. Hoori Kalamkarian and colleagues note in chapter 5 that high school college access programs have primarily been designed and researched on essentialist foundations. College access programs, however, are primarily about relationships. As such, they present a mixed-method study design—social network analysis and interviews—to capture the specific contours of the college information sharing networks at two high schools. Their findings have important implications for developing college access programs in high schools.

A relational lens can also inform policies and practices in college and university settings. As Janice McCabe addresses in chapter 6, studying—typically envisioned as a solitary activity—can also be understood through a relational lens. By envisioning studying not just as an instrumental activity for higher test scores but an opportunity for students to connect with their peers, researchers and practitioners can relationally reconceptualize the college study session. Similarly, in chapter 7 Michael Lanford uses a relational analysis of a writing support program to reimagine writing development as a predominantly relational process. Centering relationships reveals important but underanalyzed components of the college experience.

Educational theorists as well as practitioners can benefit from the insights of relational sociology. Relational tenets enrich prominent theories in education and have the potential to allow educational leaders to design policies and interventions that leverage the relational embeddedness of their students. Thus, we conceptualize relational sociology as a useful tool for the advancement of theory and practice in educational research.

The Organization and Purpose of this Book

This book's structure follows the framework discussed above. Chapters 1 and 2 engage primarily with relational sociology as theory. Chapter 1 provides a general overview of relational sociology and its potential to make insightful contributions to education. Chapter 2 details the intricate methods that might be necessary to adequately capture its multilayered view of social reality. In chapter 3, the analysis provides a practical example of how relational analyses can illuminate unique insights, and chapter 4 engages significantly with sociological theories of race and begins making practical applications to college campuses and racial climates. The remaining chapters are empirical, applying relational methods to persistent challenges in educational institutions. They analyze data regarding specific components of high school and college through a relational lens. Although our book lacks an empirical focus on younger children, we intend that the theories and methods discussed here can be applicable in elementary and middle school contexts as well.

Our relational approach may be of particular value in a time where educational debates are centered on whether free-market strategies can be used to improve educational outcomes for marginalized populations. In current educational policy discourse, school choice, an idea borne out of 1980s conservatism, has fiercely reemerged. Numerous education advocates argue strongly for the ability of families to choose schools and for the expansion of attendance options beyond the traditional public school system. In so doing, they have brought essentialism to the forefront of educational discourse. A family's choices are assumed to only matter to them. Social networks are ignored. Scant attention is paid to the power dynamics that advantage some families over others in the competition for privileged access to schools.

Relational sociologists argue that social problems cannot be reduced to the effects of broken institutions or the constraints pertaining to individual choice. Entrenched social challenges—like those related to educational inequity—are more complex and interconnected. Students and families are situated in relational networks and clash with school officials in ways that shape learning. Schools also cannot be conceptualized as independent actors. A school's ability to improve is dependent on its relationship with families, neighborhood actors, and other educational institutions. Punishing a school by siphoning off its enrollment cannot compel educational growth. Educational change happens as students interact with schools and schools interact with communities. The anti-essentialist mandate of relational sociology seeks a redirection of social analyses toward transactional processes among interconnected actors.

We do not intend for this book to sort out all the issues in the application of relational sociology to the study of education. Instead, our intent is for this text to be a primer for students and scholars intrigued by the possibilities of relational approaches in educational research. Our argument is that the field has much to gain from the theories and methods presented herein. Educational inquiries for too long have been grounded in essentialist frameworks that suggest an inevitability of social processes. Instead, we put forward a theoretical foundation on which to develop solutions to educational problems that are more attentive to the relationships and power dynamics in which educational actors are situated. By training a theoretical lens directly on the relational networks that permeate academic institutions, educational researchers have the ability to examine old problems with fresh eyes.

References

Adelman, C. (2006). *The toolbox revisited: Paths to degree completion from high school through college*. Washington, DC: US Department of Education.

Anderson, E. (2000). *Code of the street: Decency, violence, and the moral life of the inner city*. New York, NY: W. W. Norton.

Bell, D. (1991). Racial realism. *Connecticut Law Review, 24*, 363.

Berger, P. L., & Luckmann, T. (1989). *The social construction of reality: A treatise in the sociology of knowledge*. New York, NY: Anchor Books.

Bloom, D. E., Hartley, M., & Rosovsky, H. (2007). Beyond private gain: The public benefits of higher education. In *International handbook of higher education*, edited by J. J. F. Forest & P. G. Altbach, 293–308. Dordrecht, Netherlands: Springer.

Bourdieu, P. (1986). The forms of capital. In *Handbook of theory and research for the sociology of education*, edited by J. G. Richardson, 241–58. New York, NY: Greenwood Press.

Bourdieu, P., & Wacquant, L. J. (1992). *An invitation to reflexive sociology*. Chicago, IL: University of Chicago Press.

Burawoy, M. (1998). The extended case method. *Sociological Theory, 16*(1), 4–33.

Coleman, J. S. (1987). The relations between school and social structure. In *The social organization of schools*, edited by M. T. Hallinan, 177–204. Boston, MA: Springer.

Collins, P. H. (2004). *Black sexual politics: African Americans, gender, and the new racism*. New York, NY: Routledge.

Crenshaw, K. (1989). Demarginalizing the intersection of race and sex: A black feminist critique of antidiscrimination doctrine, feminist theory and antiracist politics. *University of Chicago Legal Forum, 1989*(1), 139.

DiMaggio, P., & Mohr, J. (1985). Cultural capital, educational attainment, and marital selection. *American Journal of Sociology, 90*(6), 1231–61.

Dynarski, S., Libassi, C. J., Michelmore, K., & Owen, S. (2018). *Closing the gap: The effect of a targeted, tuition-free promise on college choices of high-achieving, low-income students* (NBER working paper 25349). Cambridge, MA: National Bureau of Economic Research.

Emirbayer, M. (1997). Manifesto for a relational sociology. *American Journal of Sociology, 103*(2), 281–317.

Emirbayer, M., & Goodwin, J. (1994). Network analysis, culture, and the problem of agency. *American Journal of Sociology, 99*(6), 1411–54.

Hart, B., & Risley, T. R. (1995). *Meaningful differences in the everyday experience of young American children*. Baltimore, MD: Brookes.

Kezar, A. (2006). To use or not to use theory: Is that the question? *Higher Education: Handbook of Theory and Research, 21*, 283.

Ladson-Billings, G. (1995). Toward a theory of culturally relevant pedagogy. *American Educational Research Journal, 32*(3), 465–91.

Lewis, A. E. (2003). *Race in the schoolyard: Negotiating the color line in classrooms and communities*. Brunswick, NJ: Rutgers University Press.

McDonough, P. M. (1998). *Choosing colleges: How social class and schools structure opportunity*. Albany, NY: State University of New York Press.

Oakes, J. (1985). *Keeping track*. New Haven, CT: Yale University Press.

Perna, L.W. (2000). Differences in the decision to enroll in college among African Americans, Hispanics, and Whites. *Journal of Higher Education, 71*(2), 117–41.

Perna, L. W. (2006). Studying college access and choice: A proposed conceptual model. In *Higher education handbook of theory and research*, edited by J. C. Smart, 99–157. Dordrecht, Netherlands: Springer. http://doi.org/10.1007/1-4020-4512-3_3.

Posselt, J. R., Jaquette, O., Bielby, R., & Bastedo, M. N. (2012). Access without equity: Longitudinal analyses of institutional stratification by race and ethnicity, 1972–2004. *American Educational Research Journal, 49*(6), 1074–111.

Reardon, S. F. (2011). The widening academic achievement gap between the rich and the poor: New evidence and possible explanations. In *Whither opportunity? Rising inequality, schools, and children's life chances*, edited by G. J. Duncan & R. J. Murnane, 91–116. New York, NY: Russell Sage Foundation.

Suppes, P. (1974). The place of theory in educational research. *Educational Researcher, 3*(6), 3–10.

Teranishi, R. T., & Briscoe, K. (2008). Contextualizing race: African American college choice in an evolving affirmative action era. *Journal of Negro Education, 77*(1), 15–26.

Tierney, W. G., & Kolluri, S. (2018). Mapping the terrain. In *Diversifying digital learning: Online literacy and educational opportunity*, edited by W. G. Tierney, Z. B. Corwin, & A. Ochsner, 1. Baltimore, MD: Johns Hopkins University Press.

Tyson, K. (Ed.). (2011). *Integration interrupted: Tracking, Black students, and acting White after* Brown. Oxford, UK: Oxford University Press.

US Census Bureau. (2015). Educational attainment in the United States. Retrieved from https://www.census.gov/content/dam/Census/library/publications/2016/demo/p20-578.pdf.

Chapter 1

Toward a Relational Sociology of Education

SUNEAL KOLLURI AND WILLIAM G. TIERNEY

The social nature of humankind was a central theme of early modernist thought. For Karl Marx, what men and women produce for others is what sets them apart from animals. "An animal only produces what it immediately needs for itself or its young. It produces one-sidedly, whilst man produces universally" (Marx 1844, 4). Emile Durkheim emphasized the nature of people to collectively define norms and beliefs in moments of shared "effervescence" (1995). Similar to Marx, Durkheim argued that humanity's cooperative social capacity distinguished "man" and animal. For these foundational thinkers, social norms and structures determined social reality. Interpersonal relationships within the larger structures were mostly overlooked. Individual people, defined by their position in society, operated according to externally determined norms of interaction.

Much modern sociology has pushed back against social determinism by emphasizing the individual or at least incorporating human agency within the idea of structure. Methodological individualism and its logical extension, rational choice theory, for example, emphasize the individual as the unit of analysis. Social realities are thus assumed to be the product of individual decision making aimed at utility maximization (Tan 2014). Breaking from seminal thinkers such as Marx and Durkheim, scholars of methodological individualism and rational choice theory have emphasized the individual over the collective.

Over the past three decades, a branch of sociology has developed to think in a different manner from both of these perspectives. Relational sociology was conceived by scholars frustrated with what they viewed as an incomplete accounting of social reality. Torn between structural rigidity on one hand and methodological individualism on the other, relational sociologists have sought new units of analysis that prioritize neither a self-maintaining social structure nor an individual rationality of *Homo economicus*. Instead, they have argued, social reality is manufactured through relationships. People are who they are, and society is what it is because of the networks that social beings build among themselves. This framework formed the basis for a relational sociology that challenged traditional approaches to the study of social questions. The resulting body of work has provided the sociological literature with innovative perspectives on important social challenges (e.g., Desmond 2014; Tilly 1998).

Despite a robust movement in sociology toward a relational approach, no parallel body of work has arisen in the field of education. Our purpose here is to apply a relational lens to educational research and suggest how such a perspective might be useful to the field. We offer an outline of a theory of relational sociology and consider how it might challenge existing theoretical frameworks in education. We then consider how research methodologies in education might adopt relational principles. We argue that educational research has much to benefit from explicitly adopting the tenets of relational sociology, and in many respects, the field of education is a particularly robust arena for using these concepts.

The Theory of Relational Sociology

Relational sociology entails three core tenets: (1) a rejection of essentialist analyses of social realities that are static and detached from socio-temporal contexts, (2) a transcendence of dualities of sociological thought, and (3) a theoretical commitment to Pierre Bourdieu's concept of "field" which, as we elaborate, takes into account the idea of agency.

A Rejection of Essentialism

Relational sociologists define essentialism as an association of social phenomena with fixed characteristics. Such characteristics might inhere in individuals or social institutions. Essentialism presents "a vision of the world as a vast collection of isolated entities stacked side by side like so many jarred specimens on laboratory shelves" (Desmond 2014, 551). In "Manifesto for a Relational Sociology," Mustafa Emirbayer (1997) persuasively argues for a transactional approach to sociological research. Transactions are joint activities between people that cannot be separated into component parts without losing meaning inherent in the transaction.

Whereas relational theory rejects an emphasis on individual characteristics, it does not completely eschew categories. Categories are necessary, but they are malleable and sociotemporally defined. Emirbayer (1997) calls on relational approaches to "unfreeze static, substantialist categories that deny the fluidity of figurational patternings. . . . Essentialist modes of thinking all too often see individuals and collectivities as possessing singular, unitary 'identities' rooted in race, class, gender, or sexuality" (308). Relational thinking does not seek to diminish the importance of categories to the construction of social meaning but recasts them as a function of relationships and transactions in society.

Relational tenets apply to characteristics of individual people and social phenomena. At an individual level, one's identity is not an innate characteristic manifested in appearance, personality, or cultural beliefs but is selected from a "bundle" of selves given past experiences and present social networks (White 1992). Identities are in constant flux, constructed from relationships, as opposed to a person holding intrinsic characteristics. Relational sociologists also view social phenomena as relational processes. For example, Charles Tilly (1998) conceptualizes inequality as a societal process as opposed to a state of being. Inequality results from a deliberate set of actions made possible by enduring social structures. All of this conveys a world where a particular societal or individual characteristic is more verb than adjective.

Relational sociologists differentiate transactional approaches from "variable-centered" interactional analyses. They argue that researchers too often attribute social reality to the interacting characteristics of people rather than the relationships among them. Emirbayer (1997) explains that in relational sociology, "a dynamic, unfolding process, becomes the primary unit of analysis rather than the constituent elements themselves" (287). In quantitative analyses, researchers often study how variables "interact" to produce social outcomes. For relational sociologists, variables do not necessarily drive causal relationships. Instead, variables change. Societies are constructed of people situated in webs of social networks continually affecting one another. An essentialist sociological inquiry might study how people's personal characteristics affect their social realities; a relational sociologist more likely will address how people's social networks shape their personal characteristics. While positivist sociologists view the world in terms of causal arrows, relational sociologists view it in terms of messy, mutually reinforcing webs of interpersonal relationships.

Many of the concepts of relational sociology were built on foundations laid by John Dewey and Arthur F. Bentley. Emirbayer's "Manifesto" relies heavily on a little-known correspondence between Dewey and Bentley, "The Knowing and the Known" (1960). Like Emirbayer, they argue for the primacy of "transaction" over essentialist variables in sociological inquiry by considering the following example:

> If we watch a hunter with his gun go into a field where he sees a small animal already known to him by name as a rabbit, then, within the framework of half an hour and an acre of land, it is easy . . . to report the shooting that follows in an interactional form in which rabbit and hunter and gun enter as separates and come together by way of cause and effect. If, however, we take enough of the earth and enough thousands of years, and watch the identification of rabbit gradually taking place, arising first in the sub-naming processes of gesture, cry, and attentive movement, wherein both rabbit and hunter participate, and continuing on various levels of description and naming, we shall soon see the transaction account as the one that best covers the ground. (141)

A rabbit and hunter do not exist by nature of physical, static attributes. Rather, a process of relational configurations and transactions has constructed the social relationship in which they are wholly engaged. Social reality is thus conceived as a process of transactions that take place between people and among societies.

Importantly for the purposes of our argument on the value of relational sociology in schools, Dewey also contributed to educational theory. In *Democracy in Education* (1916), he frames learning as a profoundly relational endeavor. "Not only does social life demand teaching and learning for its own permanence, but the very process of living together educates . . . A man really living alone (alone mentally as well as physically) would have little or no occasion to reflect upon his past experience to extract its net meaning" (Dewey 1916, 5). As such, Dewey contends, schools must reflect social realities and ground themselves in the authentic experiences of students, empowering them to interpret and engage meaningfully with their social worlds. He defines education as the "reconstruction or reorganization of experience which adds to the meaning of experience, and which increases ability to direct the course of subsequent experience" (1916, 49). The learning process described by Dewey, more than forty years before his correspondence with Bentley, foreshadows a transactional approach to understanding education. Learning is a series of social interactions designed to better understand reality, which is itself a series of social interactions. Thus, Dewey, one of the earliest and most prominent theorists of education, adopted a distinctly relational perspective.

Indeed, a vast amount of essentialist approaches to educational thinking seems to have sidestepped the relational tone of Dewey's analysis. Instead, essential characteristics of students and schools dominate as explanatory variables of phenomena. If a student cannot succeed, it is because they have been assigned any number of variables—they lack motivation, they hail from a single-parent household, or they have too few books at home. Teachers suffer from poor preparation, large class sizes, or implicit bias. Schools fail because they are poorly organized, they are under-resourced, or they adhere to capitalist ideologies. Students, teachers, and schools are defined by their essential characteristics, not as the dynamic social entities envisioned by Dewey, Bentley, and modern relational sociologists. Educational theory and practice, often undergirded by essentialism, are well positioned for a transactional turn.

A Transcendence of Dualities of Sociological Thought

Relational sociology circumvents many of the central debates of sociological thought. First, from an ontological perspective, a relational approach takes the stance that reality inheres in relationships, wherein objective and socially constructed realities interact. On one hand, individuals exist in an objective social network in which one's social position and connections determine possibilities for action. On the other hand, members construct intersubjective meanings within those networks that shape their realities. Tilly (2002) conceives of "relational realism," which accepts transactions and social networks as "real and observable," but permits researchers to determine the extent to which socially constructed, symbolic meanings frame social reality. Thus, relational sociology provides a paradigmatic venue through which scholars might "transcend the realist-constructivist divide" (Mische 2014).

Second, although sociologists have long debated whether agency or social structure controls human action, relational sociology merges the two viewpoints. Relational sociologists suggest a mutual causality of macro- and micro-social realities. Randall Collins (1981), a social theorist who laid some of the cornerstones of relational sociology, argues in "On the Microfoundations of Macrosociology" that human action is not indelibly confined by an unchanging social structure. Rather, a person's social interactions construct a life path that informs their future behavior. Interpersonal transactions construct a social ecology, and that ecology, in turn, influences future transactions. Mische (2014) adds that although structural conditions allow access to some networks and restrict access to others, individual agents can strategically select which of their networks to activate to achieve particular purposes. This conception mirrors White's (1992) vision of identity, wherein one constructs a self via the "netdoms"—networks within particular social domains—in which they are situated. As Mische notes, relational thinking is a way to "overcome stale antinomies between structure and agency through a focus on the dynamics of social interactions in different kinds of social settings" (2011, 1).

The realist-constructionist and structure-agency debates occur within the confines of essentialism. Realism posits that realities are predetermined and operate independently of individual or collective meaning making. Constructionism meanwhile suggests that individual interpretations ("typifications") guide understanding and action in the social world (Berger & Luckmann 1989). Whether social realities inhere inside or outside of the human mind, they are portrayed by realists and constructionists as inert essences of human experience. Analyses that highlight structure or agency are also grounded in essentialism. If social problems are structural, groups and individuals are statically positioned within a social hierarchy. If social problems relate to individual agency, people are often assigned static attributes that determine how they shape their own social realities.[1] Instead, in its unyielding emphasis on transactional social bonds, relational sociology asserts their necessarily structural and agentic nature. As people engage in transactions, they operate within an objective social structure and actively construct social realities with others in their social networks.

As such, relational theory borrows from Marxist structuralism as well as symbolic interactionism, but accepts neither as complete. To relational theorists, structures objectively determine an actor's social position, and his or her social position determines the potential for particular relational transactions. Unlike Marx, relational theorists are not entirely systemic. They do not define individuals solely by their social positions (Emirbayer 1997). Instead, cultural meaning making takes place at the micro level, and relational processes are informed by the dispositions of individual actors. Borrowing from Erving Goffman (1959), dynamic processes unfold in face-to-face interactions defined by ongoing social performance (Emirbayer 1997). However, Desmond (2014) suggests that Goffman's adherents might get too bogged down in the particular nuances of individual interactions, neglecting the social and historical structures that have shaped them. While structural and symbolic interactionist frameworks offer important insights to relational theory, relational sociologists represent themselves as a "third approach" that holds neither to a completely "systemic" nor to a "dispositional" framework (Desmond 2014).

Educational research, much like social science research more generally, has struggled to emerge from the debates that relational approaches aim to overcome. Ontological and epistemological differences are often viewed as irreconcilable. Positivist and constructionist educational researchers remain entrenched in their ivory towers. Indeed, paradigmatic controversies between qualitative and quantitative scholars have spanned decades (e.g., Guba & Lincoln 2005; Lincoln & Guba 1985). In addition, much research on schools has been stuck on either side of the agency-structure divide. From the agency perspective, early American theorist Horace Mann's conception of education as "the great equalizer" (Mann 1848) remains salient today, even finding its way into a 2011 speech by recent Secretary of Education Arne Duncan (Rhode, Cooke, & Himanshu-Ojha 2012). However, many social reproduction theorists deny the existence of educational agency. Bowles and Gintis (1976) suggest that schools work to ensure social reproduction, and individual students can do little if anything to alter their social standing in the face of repressive academic institutions. Bourdieu (1973, 1986) conceives of distinct forms of capital—social and cultural—as subtle means by which dominant groups reify their social position. The scholarly cacophony surrounding realism, constructivism, structure, and agency represents for educational theorist Henry Giroux (1983) "a failure that has plagued educational research and practice for decades" (7). Educational research could benefit from a "relational realism" that adopts a flexible ontology and remains sensitive to the interplay of social structures and human agency.

A Theoretical Commitment to Bourdieu's Concept of Field

Although Bourdieu's work has frequently been used in analyzing educational issues, his concept of field is an often overlooked element of his theoretical framework, but it is central to relational sociology. A field is a network of individuals and institutions governed by particular power dynamics and rules of practice (Musoba & Baez 2009). For Bourdieu, a society is not a monolithic entity but is divided by a subset of fields, each with unique norms of interaction. A field is "a relational configuration endowed with a specific gravity" (Bourdieu & Wacquant 1992, 19) wherein particular forces consistently structure social interactions. A field is also a "space of conflict and competition." Dynamics of power are continually contested but stable, since some people are more equipped than others to benefit from existing social arrangements. Last, fields are not delineated by clear boundaries. For example, one does not necessarily leave the field of education when stepping off a school campus. The limits of a field's "specific gravity" need to be investigated empirically. Ultimately, Bourdieu contends that a field—its specific gravity, power dynamics, and amorphous boundaries—offers particular social rewards dispersed according to collectively understood rules that privilege some members and disadvantage others.

Fields value different forms of cultural capital. Bourdieu's analyses (1973, 1986) typically emphasize professional fields and educational fields, where those well versed in dominant cultural norms can most effectively gain access to limited resources. He thus argues that the cultural capital developed in dominant cultural households ensures the generational transmission of social advantages. A classic study by Annette Lareau (2003) illustrates how parents from middle- and upper-class households are able to more effectively support their students given the extent to which the values of the school aligned with their own. However, more recent analyses of cultural capital suggest fields wherein nondominant cultural capital is valued over dominant forms. For example, Prudence Carter (2003) identifies "Black cultural capital," pointing out cultural spaces wherein knowledge of African American styles, norms, and cultural codes enable advancement in the field. Such cultural capital, though valued within fields of hip-hop or "the street," would most likely not be useful in a university science course or a job interview at a Fortune 500 company. Fields and their corresponding capital represent an important element of relational investigations.

Central to the concept of field in relational sociology is the notion of power. Relational sociology operates within contested realms where power dynamics exist and struggles unfold (Desmond 2014). Social processes are inexorably shaped by an objective balance of power between actors in a field. Relational sociology's attention to power dynamics sets it apart from traditional social constructionist investigations. From a social constructionist perspective, social structures are the outcome of collective "typifications"—reified understandings of social norms, roles, and processes—that have become institutionalized in a society (Berger & Luckmann 1989). An objective social reality develops among a mass of interacting social actors, and each social actor plays a role in the structuring of society. Bourdieu (1991) has critiqued such a stance as an "oblivion of power" where theorizing of social reality overlooks the objective, historical conditions that privilege some and disadvantage others. Instead, Bourdieu contends that the dispositions people develop (their habitus) and the cultural capital they accumulate depend on objective social, economic, and historical conditions. Habitus and cultural capital structure power dynamics and determine social outcomes. Objective power imbalances are thus foundational to the construction of social reality in fields, a stance that relational sociologists apply to their analyses of social phenomena.

Fields also become a central unit of analysis of relational sociology because they eschew an essentialist interpretation of social boundaries. Relational inquiries emphasize how social actors construct relational linkages based on the social domains in which they engage. Relational sociologists aim to investigate social phenomena by following social networks across their fields. As such, the boundaries of relational sociology are defined not by the limits of a group or place but by the edges of social connections that define the field of inquiry (Emirbayer 1997). Thus, the symbolic interactionist who embeds him- or herself in the rich but contained space of an interpersonal or group social exchange may certainly be in "the weeds" of sociological inquiry but is largely blind to the nature of the field that has given these weeds their particular character. Much of sociology investigates specific people and places where clearly delineated in- and out-group members exist. Relational sociology, however, investigates fields—where what falls inside or outside a line of inquiry is much less clear.

Most education research exemplifies the bounded inquiry typical of nonrelational approaches. Educational studies define students by race and socioeconomic status, clustered in schools defined by their size and demographic makeup. When focusing on students and schools, educational researchers emphasize essentialist categories to bound their sample. Such approaches are reminiscent of group- and place-based approaches that Desmond (2014) argues dominate sociological research. Relational approaches to educational research enable scholars to break the sharply delineated bounds of inquiry where one is doing a study, for example, in a school or in a neighborhood but not both. Researchers might investigate relational structures shaped by power dynamics and investigate the boundaries of social phenomena operating within Bourdieusian fields. Such approaches move us away from essentialist understandings of schools and students. In what follows, we consider how the tenets of relational sociology might be applied specifically to educational theory.

Relational Sociology and Educational Theory

Most educational scholars have yet to adopt explicitly relational approaches to educational theorizing. That is not to say that implicitly relational perspectives have been avoided in educational literature, but there remains significant potential for them to be used in educational theory. In particular, studies that attempt to understand processes of social reproduction—why students from nondominant groups persistently underperform in school or how those from privileged groups are able to maintain that privilege—have been central to scholarly educational debates. Because such theories aim to disentangle processes of stratification among groups of students, they may be well suited to relational approaches. We suggest, however, that theories of social reproduction usually only selectively incorporate relational frameworks, and more fulsome, relational approaches might be useful in future analyses.

Theories of education and social stratification typically ground their analyses at one of three levels: the structural, the organizational, or the individual. At the structural level, educational processes are inseparably intertwined with social processes. In particular, theories of education grounded in Marxist thought generally hold fast to structural analyses of schools. At the organizational level, policies, instructional practices, and cultures particular to schools compel social processes relevant to educational stratification. Organizational theory in particular has contributed to the understanding of educational processes and emphasizes the inner workings of schools. Finally, educational theories operating at the individual level evaluate school phenomena based on personal characteristics of students, parents, and teachers. At this level, we include analyses that underscore students' cognitive characteristics and student and family culture as determinative of academic outcomes. In what follows, we discuss theories in education at the structural, organizational, and individual levels and address the extent to which each adopts the relational principles of eschewing essentialism, transcending divides of structure and agency and objective and subjective realities, and analyzing fields over bounded spaces.

Structural Theories of Education

Structural theories of education tend toward essentialist analyses of schools. First, they often evaluate students and schools by fixed categories such as race, ethnicity, and socioeconomic status. They measure student outcomes against these categories and tie them to larger social forces, such as capitalism and structural racism. Thus, they explicitly privilege structure over agency and mostly privilege objective reality over social construction. Given the amorphous character of what constitutes "social structure," however, structural analyses often operate in fields as opposed to bounded spaces. Economic and racial hegemony seep into educational institutions from outside, thus compelling structural researchers to broaden their educational analyses. While structural theories primarily use essentialist analyses, the commitment to field brings to the fore the ways educational processes are relational, connecting to the social phenomena operating beyond school walls.

For the sake of illustration, consider *Schooling in Capitalist America* by Samuel Bowles and Herbert Gintis (1976). Central to that book's analysis is correspondence theory, which argues that schools re-create social hierarchies because they "correspond" with capitalist institutions. The capitalist system, they argue, needs stratification to ensure that most students end up in the abundant menial positions that sustain capitalism. Using historical examples, Bowles and Gintis (1976) usefully demonstrate how capitalist institutions and the power dynamics associated with them influence the development of stratification mechanisms in schools. More recent work by critical scholars emphasizes how capitalist influences hold sway over educational institutions (Anyon 2011).

From a relational perspective, Bowles and Gintis (1976) present a theory of schools that is hamstrung by a predominantly essentialist framework. The categories employed are substances, not bonds. Wealth and poverty—not people—are their units of analysis. Such an approach invites

Emirbayer's (1997) criticisms of "variable-centered" research, wherein "it is the variable attributes themselves that 'act,' that supply initiative" (286). Also, the correspondence principle is explicitly structural. The agentic intentions of individual actors are overridden by a capitalist superstructure, and economic oppression is an objective reality with little room for cultural meaning making. As opposed to the relational call to emphasize the "microfoundations of macrosociology" (Collins 1981), Bowles and Gintis draw the causal arrow firmly in the other direction, such that the macro-structure defines interpersonal interactions. Neglecting these relational components conveys a static and hopeless portrayal of education in the United States.

Where Bowles and Gintis have contributed significantly to educational understanding is in the most relational component of their analysis: how school and corporate structures interact in the field of capitalism. They were among the first to explain in great detail how capitalist interests infiltrate United States schools and how schools in turn buttress capitalism. They present capitalism as a process affecting schools that does not locate itself in particular groups or places but in the intersecting fields of business and education. More recent scholars have since built on their analysis. Anyon (1997) famously argues in *Ghetto Schooling* that "attempting to fix inner-city schools without fixing the city in which they are embedded is like trying to clean the air on one side of a screen door" (168). Similarly, David Berliner (2005, 2013) expands our view of educational inequality to structural forces of poverty operating beyond the classroom walls. Lareau (2003) finds that socioeconomic class patterns at-home experiences that, for middle-class students, result in a "concerted cultivation" toward academic success. In addition, critical race theory as applied to education explores the academic consequences of structural racism (Ladson-Billings & Tate 1995). These analyses are all helpful in drawing important relational connections between schools and the larger society.

More relational analyses would also highlight the dynamic, transactional processes between students, teachers, and parents that maintain—or perhaps even undermine—hierarchical structures within schools and classrooms. Indeed, some educational investigations are more relational in that they explore how structural inequities are mediated by unfolding transactions in schools. Khan (2011) frames academic privilege as a relational process that unfolds between teachers, students, and parents at an elite boarding school. He describes ways students navigate webs of social ties to develop elite cultural markers and "omnivorous" cultural tastes.

Class reproduction occurs not by brute force of a capitalist superstructure but through interactions across differently positioned social actors in the field of elite education. Engaging with race and learning, Nasir (2011) conceptualizes ethnic identities as "racialized" and entwined with perceptions about education. These racialized identities develop across relational contexts both in and out of school. Research highlighting the relational components of social structures can uncover core processes by which inequality manifests in schools. However, nuanced relational insights are often overwhelmed by the structural determinism of much critical scholarship in education.

Organizational Theories of Education

Many theorists highlight the school as an institution central to social reproduction. They suggest that schools as organizations perpetuate and reify existing social hierarchy. Although perhaps philosophically aligned with structural theorists like Bowles and Gintis, these theorists are less concerned with capitalism and structural racism and are more attuned to the policies in schools that structure hierarchy along racial and socioeconomic lines. With respect to relational sociology, the potential strengths and shortcomings of such theories are the mirror image of structural inquiries. Theories of schools as organizations can forgo essential categories in favor of relational processes. In particular, a framework grounded in schools as organizations has the capacity to investigate student and staff social networks and analyze how they shape educational phenomena. Also, school-level theories have the capacity to bridge divides of structure and agency, highlighting objective circumstances in which schools are situated as well as strategies and socially constructed meanings developed by school actors. However, institutionalist frameworks that highlight the organizational structures of schools often neglect what occurs beyond their reach and ignore the complex, power-laden fields in which schools operate.

The theory of organizational culture has been applied to schools and provides a useful analytical lens through which to understand the relational capacity of organizational theory in education. Some analyses of organizational cultures highlight processes and negotiate between objective and subjective realities (Martin 2001). However, they operate explicitly within the boundaries of the organization. In the scholarly literature on schools, analyses of school culture abound. Schools can have "college going cultures" (Corwin & Tierney 2007), "professional cultures" (Lieberman

1988), "collaborative school cultures" (Waldron & McLeskey 2010), each contributing to the capacity of that school to interrupt patterns of inequity. Although these assessments of school culture might underscore important social processes and capture objective and constructed realities, they often overlook the importance of field to relational processes. Situating school culture exclusively on school campuses is incomplete from a relational perspective. First, such an approach neglects the relational networks of school actors that expand outside of the school. Second, schools themselves operate within organizational fields consisting of other schools and community organizations that are likely to affect their cultures.

Researching schools as organizations necessitates an incorporation of "field-wide relations" (Emirbayer & Johnson 2008, 38) that elevates the organizational embeddedness of educational institutions and the interpersonal networks of their social actors. Certainly, some organizational theorists have begun to investigate organizations and schools as they are situated in fields. Scott (2000) argues that institutions adapt to multiple external pressures that shape their organizational environments. He urges the "move from a generalized to a differentiated model of instructional contexts: from a conception of *the* institutional environment to one of multiple alternative institutional environments" (167). Seeing schools as part of larger "ecologies" has been a useful addition to the educational literature. Arum (2000) makes the case that scholarship in the sociology of education has redefined "school community" to encompass field relations beyond school walls.

The relational notion of field entails more than one institution's interaction with another. Fields are also interlaced with power dynamics that structure the positions within them. Habitus and cultural capital frame the ways particular organizations engage in the field. While early applications of organizational theory did not engage with habitus and capital, "new institutionalism" has encouraged the use of Bourdieusian concepts in organizational theory (DiMaggio & Powell 1991). However, Emirbayer and Johnson (2008) criticize most applications of new institutional theory for their "piecemeal" adoption of Bourdieu and suggest a more thorough incorporation of Bourdieusian notions like cultural capital and habitus into organizational analyses. While the same criticism may be leveled at research on schools as organizations, some organizational analyses have begun to emerge that situate schools in their wider organizational contexts. An important example is the concept of "organizational habitus," described by McDonough (1997) as how a school's socioeconomic environment influences its policies regarding connecting students with colleges. Other scholars have also employed the framework of organizational habitus to assess the ways schools educate their students and engage with other organizations in the larger community (Diamond, Randolph, & Spillane 2004; Horvat & Antonio 1999). The conception of the organization as an enactor of a particular habitus and embedded in field-wide relations is a nascent and promising direction for organizational research in education.

Individual Theories of Education

A substantial body of literature in education centers on the individual as the primary unit of analysis. School outcomes are assessed as stemming from the characteristics of students, teachers, or families. In isolation, such an approach falls short of a relational understanding of educational processes. Relational analyses assume that reality inheres not in the individual but in the social ties that interlace them with their social setting. A theoretical gaze focusing on the substances of people blurs their social networks. In addition, although individual theories have the capacity to blend structure and agency, objective and subjective realities, they typically remain entrenched on one end of the spectrums. Individualistic theories emphasize structure or agency and objective truths or subjective meanings. Finally, theories of education that emphasize individual characteristics overlook Bourdieu's concept of field. Though Bourdieu certainly views personal attributes as important to social processes, those attributes only gain meaning when situated in fields with particular rules and power dynamics. Educational theories grounded in the individual often take a myopic view of social reality, neglecting social networks and fields and failing to transcend the structure-agency and objective-subjective divides.

Popular in current educational discourse are Angela Duckworth's theory of grit and Carol Dweck's theory of growth mindset. Although both frameworks have offered important insights toward a better understanding of educational outcomes, from a relational perspective each is firmly immersed in essentialism and thus incapable of holistically evaluating educational processes. Duckworth, Peterson, Matthews, and Kelly (2007) construct the concept of grit around personal traits such as perseverance, passion, and an ability to delay gratification, arguing that a student's grit can predict academic outcomes. Dweck (2008) highlights the importance of cognitive characteristics to predict school success. A growth mindset is a personal approach to learning wherein students believe that intelligence is not fixed but can be developed with intellectual practice. Each theory highlights an essentialist component of students as predictive of social processes. However, grit and a growth mindset probably develop in relational contexts. A student naturally endowed with grit and a growth mindset may see intellectual growth stunted by a disempowered social position and an unsupportive social network. Theories like these, grounded in cognitive psychology, will inevitably fall short of a holistic understanding of a highly relational educational world.

Alternatively, social cognitive theory (Bandura 1977, 2001) situates cognition in social environments, moving the psychology of education closer to relational sociology. Bandura emphasizes self-efficacy and agency as characteristics of students who feel capable of shaping their social worlds. His concept of collective efficacy widens the social frame even more, emphasizing that people operate in social systems, and these systems provide modes of interaction that allow for people to affect their environments in a collective fashion (Bandura 2001). One's sense of collective efficacy acts in conjunction with their individual agency. For example, in assessing personal efficacy, "a football quarterback obviously considers the quality of his offensive line, the fleetness and blocking capabilities of his running backs, the adeptness of his receivers, and how well they all work together" (Bandura 2000, 76).

A social cognitive approach certainly begins to elevate social bonds over individual essences. However, the theory largely neglects structural influences and field-related power dynamics, core components of relational analyses. Collins (1981) brings cognitive processes more fully into the relational realm. His concept of interaction ritual chains suggests that reality is symbolically encoded in human cognition by way of micro-situations that elicit emotional responses. Power is thus constructed relationally, as situational interactions compel psychological responses and create and reify coalitions. Behaviors are made routine by way of repeated interactions and these behaviors produce and reproduce the norms and structures of a social space. Thus, relational sociology stretches the bounds of social psychology by looking at social interactions as the drivers of larger social processes.

Other theories emphasizing the individual highlight culture over cognition—and perhaps begin to theorize fields and structures in education. Prominent among cultural theories of education is John Ogbu's (1978) theory of oppositional culture. Ogbu argues that certain students assume oppositional outlooks because they view themselves as "involuntary minorities," brought or conquered into this country by no choice of their own. Oppositional identities are a cultural defense mechanism adopted by African Americans and Latinx people in oppressive school contexts. These identities are developed as a collective ethos among particular marginalized groups and are reinforced by parents in the household (Ogbu & Simons 1998). Ogbu does not deny the impact of structural inequality, but for him, it is not the primary driver of persistent educational inequality. Rather, historical racism acts as a weight dragging down the aspirations of those within nondominant cultural communities. Ogbu's theory of cultural oppositionality has come to "dominate contemporary discussions of the links between culture and ethnic and racial stratification in education" (Warikoo & Carter 2009).

The essentialist nature of oppositional culture theory drives its shortcomings. For Ogbu, culture is embedded in individuals by historical realities independent of their agency. Thus, cultural behaviors are an essential and objective reality for students from "involuntary minority" communities. Also, Ogbu's unit of analysis is culture, and his analysis is bounded within cultural spaces—primarily families and peer groups. As such, the theory largely overlooks how schools and other institutions within the field of education might influence social realities. Oppositional culture is widely criticized for neglecting how school policies and structures marginalize students from nondominant cultures (Lewis & Diamond 2015; Mickelson 1990; Tyson 2011). A theory of oppositional identities would benefit from a more relational analysis. Students who are oppositional must have someone to oppose, and a more relational conceptualization of oppositional culture might more accurately reflect educational patterns for African American and Latinx youth.

Some educational scholarship weaves cognitive and cultural considerations to situate learning processes in more relational contexts. In particular, theories of critical and culturally relevant pedagogy emphasize how student networks across schools, homes, and communities influence learning. Giroux (1983) seeks to blur the line between agency and structure in developing a theory of resistance in schools. He emphasizes that students generate ideologies of resistance from families, communities, and peers. He also challenges essentialist notions of resistance, arguing that resistance behavior can be "both underlying the structure of social domination and containing the logic necessary to overcome it" (1983, 31). Ladson-Billings (1995), meanwhile, elevates cultural concerns of individual student engagement. In her influential theory on pedagogy, she adopts a Deweyan approach to learning that emphasizes student culture—social connections between students, their teachers, their peers, and their home communities. Scholars who wish to adopt a relational lens might use these frameworks in ways that eschew essentialist categories and elevate transactional processes in schools and neighborhoods.

Relational Realism in Education

Our purpose here surely has not been to lament the uselessness of nonrelational theories of educational sociology. On the contrary, these theories have provided rigorous lenses through which to investigate questions central to educational inequity, and each theory has some explanatory power. However, many fail to holistically use relational tenets. Structural theories of education often investigate fields but neglect agency, subjectivism, and relational processes. Organizational theories can be relationally robust where structural theories are not but neglect a thorough investigation of the idea of a field. Individual theories tend toward essentialism and overlook the influence of fields. While some education scholars operating at each of these levels have prompted theoretical thrusts in a relational direction, relational shortcomings remain, leaving educational scholarship wanting. Our understanding of educational inequity and social reproduction is incomplete because of the dearth of theory that engages with relational reality.

Relational sociology seeks to recast the social world from one primarily analyzed in terms of individual and collective essence to one of ongoing social transaction among connected social actors. Such an approach may prove particularly useful to educational investigations. Students interact with peers, families, and teachers, who occupy very different positions in the social structure. A relational approach to educational theory highlights transactional processes over essences, assesses the interaction of objective structures and socially constructed meanings, and theorizes fields as opposed to bounded categories of places or groups. Such a theory may necessitate transcending structural, organizational, and individual boundaries that typically confine educational thought to an essentialist social reality. However, this theoretical approach to education may call for new methods in education research. We turn now to an analysis of how relational methodologies might be employed to deepen educational knowledge.

Relational Sociology and Methodology in Education

What might be the lineaments of a framework for undertaking relational studies in education? Relational researchers need to (1) investigate dynamic social ties over individual essences as their units of analysis, (2) emphasize processes that bring about conflict or harmony among social actors, and (3) explore fields with amorphous boundaries. Incorporating these tenets is certainly possible across the methodological diversity of sociological research but might differ for quantitatively and qualitatively oriented researchers. Admittedly, we are making a stark division between quantitative and qualitative methods. We use them each as ideal types to assess the relational capacity of research in education.

Quantitative Methods in Education

Quantitative research can make use of the above relational tenets. Data collection in education research typically involves an exploration of variables that measure students' personal characteristics, social circumstances, and academic outcomes, but a relational approach also necessitates the investigation of social ties. At a minimum, egocentric analyses that assess the types of people with whom a particular student interacts might be measured against variables of interest. In addition, quantitative analyses seeking relational insight require longitudinal data to holistically encapsulate social processes. Relationships, like the social world, are inherently dynamic, and cross-sectional data conceal relational and social dynamism. Finally, confining quantitative research within a bounded space is inappropriate for uncovering relational processes that span beyond institutional boundaries. Research on a particular school, class, or group of students with a shared characteristic might neglect important connections that extend beyond the confines of the research.

Quantitative methodologies in educational inquiries often fall short of relational understandings. Approaches employing primarily multiple regression or hierarchical linear modeling techniques, however useful from one vantage point, will be seen to emphasize essentialist characteristics over social ties and patterns over processes. Students are of low or high socioeconomic status, are low- or high-achieving, are White or non-White, or are in a treatment group or outside of a treatment group. They are nested in schools that may also be low or high socioeconomic status, low- or high-achieving, predominantly White or non-White, or treated or untreated by an intervention. Characteristics of students and schools are predictive of other characteristics of students and schools. The nuanced relational networks that drive social processes occurring on school campuses remain underinvestigated.

A relational approach eschews a heavy emphasis on essentialist categories of students, their schools, and their families and instead investigates academic outcomes as a process that is influenced by students' dynamic social networks. By necessity, categorical attributes are at the center of quantitative investigations. Certainly important advancements in our understanding of educational challenges are continually made by quantitative investigations of students and schools. Although such inquiries illustrate many important patterns that occur in schools, they do little to delineate relational processes central to social reality.

Qualitative Methods in Education

Qualitative methods are well suited to exploring social ties, processes, and fields. Through interviews, case studies, or ethnography, qualitative researchers can apply tenets of relational sociology to research in schools. Relational research methods seek to highlight connections between school actors beyond the meanings the research subjects have developed for themselves. They seek to understand how members from different social positions either come into conflict or achieve harmony and produce new social realities at the school. Relational qualitative work in education also transcends traditional boundaries of educational inquiry, expanding research beyond classrooms and into homes and neighborhoods.

Qualitative methodologies in education, although more inclusive of relational principles, generally fall short of fully encompassing the aforementioned methodological strategies. For example, research relying heavily on interviews investigates phenomena from the perspective of individuals, understating the potential influence of their social networks. Educational ethnography is often bounded by predetermined essentialist student categories, such as the schools they attend, courses they take, or characteristics they share. Once an ethnographic object has been determined, the bounded sample is investigated for its existing properties of interest. Ethnographers thus study school cultures as one might study a colorful aquarium tank—the fish have evolved, but little attention is given to their continuing evolution. The ethnographer dutifully constructs a "thick description" (Geertz 1973) of essences, symbols, and intricacies of an already developed ecosystem.

A relational perspective laments the compartmental and static character of much educational ethnography. Take, for example, the important ethnographic work of Paul Willis (1977), who exemplifies how educational ethnographies partially adopt a relational framework. In *Learning to Labor*, Willis endeavors to address the question of "how working class kids get working class jobs" (1977, 1). The question deals explicitly with a process, and Willis's investigation extends to the field of social reproduction that operates outside of the school. His work investigates the boys, their parents, and their teachers and captures how cultural conflict unfolds among teachers and students. Thus, Willis's ethnography engages, at least in part, with social networks, cultural conflict, and field.

However, the actors involved in *Learning to Labor* are understood for their essences. The "lads" are troublemakers, committed to undermining their teachers and their own educational opportunities. The ear'oles, also from working-class backgrounds, are the do-gooders juxtaposed against the lads for their willingness to engage respectfully with their teachers and schoolwork. How one chooses to become a lad or an ear'ole remains unclear. Willis treats becoming a lad as an essential, defining moment and overlooks the dynamic and varying processes it might entail. He thus falls into the trap of essentialism. He sacrifices an in-depth analysis of how social ties draw students toward one group or the other for a static presentation of two groups whose agency is undermined by their predetermined labels. The static construction of these social groups belies the relational processes that likely created them. Willis's work is exemplary and makes meaningful contributions to educational research. However, much like other qualitative academic inquiry in education, his investigation would benefit from a more holistically relational approach.

Thus, qualitative and quantitative approaches to studying schools have neglected to fully encompass the tenets of relational sociology. We ask, then, what methodological approaches might supplement traditional quantitative and qualitative inquiries to enhance their relational capacities?

Two central methodological approaches have been associated with relational sociology. Social network analysis is a quantitative method grounded in social relations. While traditional quantitative approaches to social research analyze how essential characteristics of individuals predict particular outcomes, social network analyses assess how one's presence and position in a group of people might influence realities. Social network analysts map webs of social relationships to understand their complex and dynamic patterns. The analyst can uncover how the structural dynamics affect individuals and the group itself (Wasserman & Faust 1994). From a more qualitative lens, relational ethnography has emerged as an alternative to ethnographic inquiries that emphasize substantialist characteristics of social objects. Whereas ethnographies typically study essences of individuals housed in their bounded institutions, relational approaches emphasize social transactions of individuals embedded in their fields. Both methods offer new and helpful means for investigating education but have limitations that should be heeded by educational researchers using relational techniques. To demonstrate what are admittedly abstract concepts, we turn to a detailed discussion of these methodologies, how they adopt relational tenets, and how they might be used in educational settings.

Social Network Analysis

Employing sophisticated mathematical techniques, social network analysis represents a developing approach to studying how relationship structures are associated with social outcomes. By relationship structures, we have in mind the interpersonal connections through which information might pass or social phenomena might unfold. The methodology seeks to represent social relationships via graphic models wherein social actors, represented by nodes, are connected by lines to people they identify as part of their social network. Social network analysts employ graph theory and matrix calculations to analyze social data (Scott 2000) and seek to understand how network configurations might predict social outcomes. For example, Mark Granovetter (1977) evaluated how the ties in one's social network predict employment information sharing; Nancy Howell Lee (1969) researched how women find an abortion provider; Thomas Valente (1996) observed how innovations diffuse across a society; and Nicholas Christakis and James Fowler (2008) evaluated smoking patterns among clusters of social ties. Social network theory is a quantitative application of relational sociology, but questions have arisen regarding whether applications of network analysis have been able to holistically capture relational social realities.

A few prominent relational theorists assert the potential of social network analysis to concretely measure and evaluate patterns of relational data. For Charles Tilly (2002), network analysis represents a valid methodological application of a relational realist ontology that can highlight interdependent social structures. White (1963) suggests that mapping complex social networks can outline social structures and illuminate understandings that remain obscured in traditional cultural investigations. Social network analyses unearth social structures and processes that have the ability to transcend the individual consciousness of actors and investigators (Lorrain & White 1971, 50). Emirbayer and Goodwin (1994) praise social network analysis for providing usable techniques to investigate what had previously been confined to metaphorical analyses of abstract networks in amorphous fields. Whereas previous investigations relied on symbolic understandings conveyed by social actors through qualitative interviews and ethnographic observations, social network methodologies provide concrete maps of social structures and variables that can add clarity to elements of social reality underanalyzed by ethnographic investigations. In addition, social network analyses arose in contradistinction to dominant statistical methodologies of the mid-twentieth century. Their focus on tangible interactional fields is a quantitative response to the statistical analyses developed in the late 1940s that directed sociological inquiry toward the individual as the primary unit of analysis (Emirbayer and Goodwin 1994).

In their detailed analysis of the relational capacity of social network analysis, Emirbayer and Goodwin (1994) suggest certain limitations of the method. They question the extent to which existing network analyses have highlighted the importance of cultural symbols and individual agency. "Network analysis gains its purchase on the social structure only at the considerable cost of losing its conceptual grasp upon culture, agency, and process" (Emirbayer & Goodwin 1994, 1447). Regarding culture, Emirbayer and Goodwin contend that cultural narratives and meanings are essential for constructing social realities. Social network analyses, steeped in network structures, tend to overlook how cultural formations penetrate social reality independently of a social network. Regarding agency, the authors assert that network analyses overemphasize structure. Often, they argue, methodologies that overstress social structure will neglect "the dynamic efforts and projects of historical actors" (1446). Social network analysis, while having developed valuable tools for relational sociology, has struggled to adequately account for culture and agency.

Despite these shortcomings, social network techniques can offer unique insights into school structures and processes. Scholars of education have only just begun to apply social network techniques to schools. Carolan (2013) posits that educational scholarship has been slow to incorporate social network analysis because of the preeminence of psychological theories that have guided the discipline, the desire of educational scholars to elevate their research as science, and the proliferation of data software that uses statistical regression, a technique poorly suited to network analyses. Given the extent to which students build social connections with teachers, peers, and community members, however, education would be an appropriate realm in which to apply social network analysis. Frank (1998) argues that network theory might be combined with hierarchical linear modeling to more accurately capture school culture, wherein students nested in classrooms construct social networks that shape their educational experiences. Despite the infrequency of network analyses in schools, some recent studies have made use of these methods. Social network analyses have assessed the network properties associated with the development of social capital at school sites among teachers (Bridwell-Mitchell & Cooc 2016) and students (Bridwell-Mitchell 2017). Au and Ferrare (2014) investigate the network connections of wealthy elites and the ways their social connections influence charter school reform in Washington. Although social network analysis has begun to make promising inroads in educational research, many relational sociologists call for approaches that more completely account for cultural meanings and processes.

Relational Ethnography

Social network analyses might neglect to highlight culture and agency, but such emphases have always been at the core of ethnographic research. Alongside recent advances in social network analysis, a conception of relational ethnography has emerged to explore the cultural and agentic components of relational phenomena. Matthew Desmond (2014) conceives of relational ethnography in contrast to traditional ethnographies, which he argues adopt essentialist conceptions of research objects. Instead, relational ethnography is transactional. It adopts "relational mechanisms"—the processes of interaction between various social actors—as units of analysis. Desmond thus adopts the perspective of the relational theorists who came before him (Collins, White, and Emirbayer) who emphasize that social reality breaks through the categorical barriers imposed by traditional social analysis. He takes aim at "group" and "place-based" ethnographies that treat objects as stationary and insular. Relational ethnographies transcend the essentialism that views society as constituted by isolated, bounded groups defined by static and coherent attributes. Desmond argues for "studying fields rather than places, boundaries rather than bounded groups, processes rather than processed people, and cultural conflict rather than group culture" (2014, 562). Moving away from preconceived, stable attributes allows for a more authentic understanding of a society defined more by its intersecting and interactive processes than by any essential characteristics.

Like other qualitative strategies—namely, the extended case method and critical ethnography—relational ethnography explores a dialectical interaction between the macro-structure and its micro-foundations. The extended case method (Burawoy 1998) calls on researchers to tie local experiences to structural and historical forces through the guidance of existing social theory. Critical ethnography aims to chronicle the unfolding of socially constructed power dynamics at the local level (Anderson 1989). Relational ethnography, however, differs from these methods. Although relational ethnography certainly engages with local experiences and power structures, it intentionally seeks out the local manifestations of a power struggle. Relational ethnography is not exclusively localized or structural but exists across a variety of localities, exploring social structures through their interpersonal and multisited dynamics. For example, instead of observing low-income students harmed by an under-resourced school, a relational ethnographer must "witness the clash firsthand" (Desmond 2014, 559). seeking out the stratified power struggles that unfold between students, teachers, and parents within and beyond school walls. For the relational ethnographer, a rigid social structure is not assumed to apply to static ethnographic subjects. Rather, continually unfolding conflicts shape a dynamic social structure.

These concepts are well illustrated by Desmond's (2016) work *Evicted.* The book won the Andrew Carnegie medal for nonfiction, was named one of the best books of the year by the *New York Times* and the *Washington Post*, and won the Pulitzer Prize for nonfiction, an unusual feat for an academic tome. Desmond immersed himself into two low-income rental markets in Milwaukee, Wisconsin—a predominantly Black neighborhood, and a majority White trailer park—to better understand the process of eviction as it unfolds between low-income renters and their landlords. The research took him into apartment buildings, trailer park offices, courthouses, a drug rehabilitation center, and a casino. The dual focus on landlords and renters across multiple sites allows for a more holistic assessment of eviction processes and the cultural conflicts that ensue. Tracking the web of rental market relationships that spans across Milwaukee and engaging deeply with the interpersonal transactions occurring there allow for relational insights of poverty and housing policy that have been unnoticed by more essentialist investigations.

Despite its advantages, conducting relational ethnography work presents logistical and theoretical barriers to holistically describing social processes. From a practical standpoint, relational ethnographers face daunting barriers to gaining entry to a relational network and engaging with each member with the depth characteristic of traditional ethnographies (Desmond 2014). From a theoretical perspective, relational ethnographers endure unique challenges of defining boundaries of a study characterized by amorphous, unclear limits. Where a relational network begins and ends is much harder to define than the outer limits of a particular school or teaching staff. In addition, although traditional ethnographies present challenges of generalization, more layers of complexity accompany the generalizability of relational ethnographies. Not only must a relational ethnographer address whether research subjects are typical of others with their characteristics, their relationships with other network members should also be assessed for representativeness of relationships within other, similar social networks (Desmond 2014). Relational ethnography provides a useful opportunity to engage with the complexity of social phenomena, but in doing so, it presents unique challenges to the ethnographer.

Most ethnographies of education incorporate relational elements. They explore bonds between students and teachers, they frequently extend inquiry to students' families and peers, and their insights often highlight conflict between students, teachers, and peers. However, relational aspects of school ethnographies are incorporated seemingly by accident and are rarely (if ever) holistically investigated. Ethnographies might investigate educational processes, but are confined neatly to a particular classroom or school campus. Alternatively, school ethnographies might extend into student homes and neighborhoods but emphasize static, essential categories of students, teachers, and schools.

The highly transactional nature of education can benefit from an explicitly relational approach. For example, studies of failure—often treated as a salient, static attribute of urban students in ethnographic research—is actually a highly transactional process that involves multiple actors at different levels, expansive boundaries, and cultural conflict. Academic identity is often treated as something students bring with them to school contexts rather than something shaped by relational processes within and beyond school walls. Relational ethnography can be used to deconstruct essentialist categories that largely define current educational research.

Though relational ethnography may sacrifice some of the methodological precision of social network analysis, it offers an enhanced capacity to explore cultural and individual meanings amid social conflict and cooperation in and beyond schools.

Educational research has not fully harnessed the capacity of either network analytical techniques or relational ethnography to address questions of import to schools. Quantitatively, a robust body of educational research makes use of statistical analyses highlighting essential characteristics of individuals and schools. Few of these studies emphasize social ties or use network analytical techniques. Also, although there exists no shortage of educational ethnographies, those analyzing fields, boundaries, and processes are rare. While certainly not the only means of understanding relational processes (see other examples later in this volume), social network analysis and relational ethnography represent useful methodologies to apply to education research.

Conclusion

The purpose here has been to outline the theoretical and methodological contributions of relational approaches to the discipline of sociology and suggest how similar contributions might be made to educational research. We first suggested that relational sociology is a meaningful theoretical contribution to a field divided by holism and methodological individualism. We then assessed ways influential educational theories adopt relational tenets and how relational approaches might be enhanced in the discipline. In particular, theories of social reproduction in education may benefit from more relational investigations that develop fuller, more nuanced analyses of school processes that compel differences in academic achievement. Finally, we addressed methodologies associated with relational sociology and where there might be room for their incorporation into research on schools, colleges, and universities.

We acknowledge that concrete guidelines for how to conduct relational sociological inquiries in education are underdeveloped. We have not intended to provide a step-by-step recipe for relational inquiry as if this were merely a cookbook for theoretical chefs. Rather, we highlighted key tenets of relational sociology to emphasize the importance of applying a relational frame to educational research. Using such a frame emphasizes dynamic social bonds over static essences that frequently overcategorize students and their schools. A relational approach engages meaningfully with structure and agency, social constructions, and objective truths to investigate how educational outcomes are the product of macro-structures as well as the actions and interpretations of educational actors. By using this framework, scholars of education will consider investigating phenomena as they occur beyond preordained bounded spaces, such as schools or classrooms. Relational investigations might provide fresh insight to stubborn patterns of educational inequity.

Our objective here has not been to assert the superiority of relational approaches over all others but to emphasize their potential to contribute interesting insights to intractable challenges in education. Some of the field's most meaningful contributions have used some relational elements, but often have highlighted the essential over the transactional, narrow ontological stances over nuanced analyses of social reality, and bounded spaces over expansive fields. Much educational research observes social processes happening in schools, teaching happening in classrooms, and learning happening in students' heads. If relational sociologists are correct that social understanding necessitates "a move from substances to networks, from essences to relations" (Desmond 2014, 575), an educational field that investigates only these neatly defined, predetermined spaces may be looking for answers in the wrong places.

Note

1. For a more relational, temporally situated analysis of agency, see Emirbayer and Mische (1998).

References

Anderson, G. L. (1989). Critical ethnography in education: Origins, current status, and new directions. *Review of Educational Research*, *59*(3), 249–70.

Anyon, J. (1997). *Ghetto schooling: A political economy of urban educational reform*. New York, NY: Teachers College Press.

Arum, R. (2000). Schools and communities: Ecological and institutional dimensions. *Annual Review of Sociology*, *26*(1), 395–418.

Au, W., & Ferrare, J. J. (2014). Sponsors of policy: A network analysis of wealthy elites, their affiliated philanthropies, and charter school reform in Washington State. *Teachers College Record*, *116*(8), 1–24.

Bandura, A. (1977). Self-efficacy: toward a unifying theory of behavioral change. *Psychological Review, 84*(2), 191.

Bandura, A. (2000). Exercise of human agency through collective efficacy. *Current Directions in Psychological Science, 9*(3), 75–78.

Bandura, A. (2001). Social cognitive theory: An agentic perspective. *Annual Review of Psychology, 52*(1), 1–26.

Berliner, D. C. (2005). Our impoverished view of educational review. *Teachers College Record, 108*(6), 949–95.

Berliner, D. C. (2013). Effects of inequality and poverty vs. teachers and schooling on America's youth. *Teachers College Record, 115*(12), 1–25.

Berger, P. L., & Luckmann, T. (1989). *The social construction of reality: A treatise in the sociology of knowledge.* New York, NY: Anchor Books.

Bourdieu, P. (1973). Cultural reproduction and social reproduction. In *Knowledge, education, and cultural change: Papers in the sociology of education*, edited by R. Brown, 71–112. London, UK: Tavistock.

Bourdieu, P. (1986). The forms of capital. In *Handbook of theory and research for the sociology of education*, edited by J. G. Richardson, 241–58. New York, NY: Greenwood Press.

Bourdieu, P. (1991). *Language and symbolic power.* Cambridge, UK: Polity.

Bourdieu, P., & Wacquant, L. J. (1992). *An invitation to reflexive sociology.* Chicago, IL: University of Chicago Press.

Bowles, S., & Gintis, H. (1976). *Schooling in capitalist America.* New York: Basic Books.

Bridwell-Mitchell, E. N. (2017). Them that's got: How tie formation in partnership networks gives high schools differential access to social capital. *American Educational Research Journal, 54*(6), 1221–55.

Bridwell-Mitchell, E. N., & Cooc, N. (2016). The ties that bind: How social capital is forged and forfeited in teacher communities. *Educational Researcher, 45*(1), 7–17.

Burawoy, M. (1998). The extended case method. *Sociological Theory, 16*(1), 4–33.

Carolan, B. V. (2013). *Social network analysis and education: Theory, methods and applications.* Thousand Oaks, CA: Sage Publications.

Carter, P. L. (2003). "Black" cultural capital, status positioning, and schooling conflicts for low-income African American youth. *Social Problems, 50*(1), 136–155.

Christakis, N. A., & Fowler, J. H. (2008). The collective dynamics of smoking in a large social network. *New England Journal of Medicine, 358*(21), 2249–58.

Collins, R. (1981). On the microfoundations of macrosociology. *American Journal of Sociology, 86*(5), 984–1014.

Corwin, Z. B., & Tierney, W. G. (2007). *Getting there—and beyond: Building a culture of college-going in high schools.* Los Angeles, CA: University of Southern California, Center for Higher Education Policy Analysis.

Desmond, M. (2014). Relational ethnography. *Theory and Society, 43*(5), 547–79.

Desmond, M. (2016). *Evicted: Poverty and profit in the American city*. New York, NY: Crown.

Dewey, J. (1916). *Democracy and education*. Chelmsford, MA: Courier.

Dewey, J., & Bentley, A. F. (1960). *Knowing and the known*. Boston, MA: Beacon Press.

Diamond, J. B., Randolph, A., & Spillane, J. P. (2004). Teachers' expectations and sense of responsibility for student learning: The importance of race, class, and organizational habitus. *Anthropology & Education Quarterly, 35*(1), 75–98.

DiMaggio, P. J., & Powell, W. W. (Eds.). (1991). *The new institutionalism in organizational analysis* (vol. 17). Chicago, IL: University of Chicago Press.

Duckworth, A. L., Peterson, C., Matthews, M. D., & Kelly, D. R. (2007). Grit: Perseverance and passion for long-term goals. *Journal of Personality and Social Psychology, 92*(6), 1087.

Durkheim, E. (1995). *The elementary forms of religious life*, translated by K. Fields. 1912; New York, NY: Free Press.

Dweck, C. S. (2008). *Mindset: The new psychology of success*. New York, NY: Random House.

Emirbayer, M. (1997). Manifesto for a relational sociology. *American Journal of Sociology, 103*(2), 281–317.

Emirbayer, M., & Goodwin, J. (1994). Network analysis, culture, and the problem of agency. *American Journal of Sociology, 99*(6), 1411–54.

Emirbayer, M., & Johnson, V. (2008). Bourdieu and organizational analysis. *Theory and Society, 37*(1), 1–44.

Emirbayer, M., & Mische, A. (1998). What is agency? *American Journal of Sociology, 103*(4), 962–1023.

Frank, K. A. (1998). Quantitative methods for studying social context in multilevels and through interpersonal relations. *Review of Research in Education, 23*(1), 171–216.

Geertz, C. (1973). Thick description: Toward an interpretive theory of culture. In C. Geertz, *The interpretation of cultures: Selected essays*, 3–30. New York, NY: Basic Books.

Giroux, H. A. (1983). *Theory and resistance in education: A pedagogy for the opposition*. South Hadley, MA: Bergin & Garvey.

Goffman, E. (1959). *The presentation of self in everyday life*. New York, NY: Anchor.

Granovetter, M. S. (1977). The strength of weak ties. In *Social networks*, 347–67. Amsterdam: Elsevier.

Guba, E. G., & Lincoln, Y. S. (2005). Paradigmatic controversies, contradictions, and emerging confluences. In *The Sage handbook of qualitative research* (3rd ed.), edited by N. K. Denzin & Y. S. Lincoln, 191–216. Thousand Oaks, CA: Sage.

Horvat, E. M., & Antonio, A. L. (1999). "Hey, those shoes are out of uniform": African American girls in an elite high school and the importance of habitus. *Anthropology & Education Quarterly, 30*(3), 317–42.

Khan, S. R. (2012). *Privilege: The making of an adolescent elite at St. Paul's School.* Princeton, NJ: Princeton University Press.

Lee, N. H. (1969). *The search for an abortionist.* Chicago, IL: University of Chicago Press.

Ladson-Billings, G. (1995). Toward a theory of culturally relevant pedagogy. *American Educational Research Journal, 32*(3), 465–91.

Ladson-Billings, G., & Tate, W. F. (1995). Toward a critical race theory of education. *Teachers College Record, 97*(1), 47.

Lareau, A. (2003). *Unequal childhoods: Class, race, and family life.* Berkeley, CA: University of California Press.

Lewis, A. E., & Diamond, J. B. (2015). *Despite the best intentions: How racial inequality thrives in good schools.* Oxford, UK: Oxford University Press.

Lieberman, A. (1988). *Building a professional culture in schools.* New York, NY: Teachers College Press.

Lincoln, Y. S., & Guba, E. G. (1985). *Naturalistic inquiry.* Thousand Oaks, CA: Sage.

Lorrain, F., & White, H. C. (1971). Structural equivalence of individuals in social networks. *Journal of Mathematical Sociology, 1*(1), 49–80.

Mann, H. (1848). Twelfth annual report to the Massachusetts Board of Education. In *The republic and the school: Horace Mann and the education of free men.* New York, NY: Teachers College Press.

Martin, J. (2001). *Organizational culture: Mapping the terrain.* London, UK: Sage.

Marx, K. (1844). Estranged labour. In *Economic and philosophical manuscripts of 1844.* Retrieved from https://www.marxists.org/archive/marx/works/1844/manuscripts/labour.htm.

McDonough, P. M. (1998). Structuring college opportunities: A cross-case analysis of organizational cultures, climates, and habiti. In *Sociology of education: Emerging perspectives*, edited by Carlos Alberto Torres & Theodore R. Mitchell, 181–210. Albany, NY: State University of New York Press.

Mickelson, R. A. (1990). The attitude-achievement paradox among Black adolescents. *Sociology of Education, 63*(1), 44–61.

Mische, A. (2014). Relational sociology, culture, and agency. In *The Sage Handbook of Social Network Analysis*, edited by J. Scott & P. J. Carrington, 80–97. London, UK: Sage.

Musoba, G., & Baez, B. (2009). The cultural capital of cultural and social capital: An economy of translations. *Higher Education: Handbook of Theory and Research, 24*, 151–82.

Nasir, N. I. (2011). *Racialized identities: Race and achievement among African American youth.* Stanford, CA: Stanford University Press.

Ogbu, J. (1978). *Minority education and caste*. New York, NY: Academic Press.

Ogbu, J. U., & Simons, H. D. (1998). Voluntary and involuntary minorities: A cultural-ecological theory of school performance with some implications for education. *Anthropology & Education Quarterly*, *29*(2), 155–88.

Rhode, D., Cooke, K., & Himanshu-Ojha (2012, 19 December). The decline of the great equalizer. *The Atlantic*. Retrieved from https://www.theatlantic.com/business/archive/2012/12/the-decline-of-the-great-equalizer/266455/.

Scott, J. (2000). *Social network analysis*. London, UK: Sage.

Tan, E. (2014). Human capital theory: A holistic criticism. *Review of Educational Research*, *84*(3), 411–45.

Tilly, C. (1998). *Durable inequality*. Berkeley, CA: University of California Press.

Tilly, C. (2002). *Stories, identities, and political change*. New York, NY: Rowman & Littlefield.

Tyson, K. (2011). *Integration interrupted: Tracking, black students, and acting white after* Brown. Oxford, UK: Oxford University Press.

Valente, T. W. (1996). Social network thresholds in the diffusion of innovations. *Social networks*, *18*(1), 69–89.

Waldron, N. L., & McLeskey, J. (2010). Establishing a collaborative school culture through comprehensive school reform. *Journal of Educational and Psychological Consultation*, *20*(1), 58–74.

Warikoo, N., & Carter, P. (2009). Cultural explanations for racial and ethnic stratification in academic achievement: A call for a new and improved theory. *Review of Educational Research*, *79*(1), 366–94.

Wasserman, S., & Faust, K. (1994). *Social network analysis: Methods and applications*. Cambridge, UK: Cambridge University Press.

White, H. C. (1963). *An anatomy of kinship: Mathematical models for structures of cumulated roles*. Englewood Cliffs, NJ: Prentice Hall.

White, H. C. (1992). *Identity and control: A structural theory of social action*. Princeton, NJ: Princeton University Press.

Willis, P. E. (1977). *Learning to labor: How working class kids get working class jobs*. New York, NY: Columbia University Press.

Chapter 2

Embedding Networks in Fields

Toward an Expanded Model of Relational Analysis in Education

JOSEPH J. FERRARE

Education is an activity constituted by relationships. These relationships define how people, practices, and ideas are brought together and kept apart in processes of learning, teaching, and policy making. To understand the factors shaping educational policies and practices thus necessitates an investigation into the constellation of relationships in which these activities are embedded. In essence, this is the central objective of relational sociology. Given this emphasis, it is not surprising that researchers are increasingly looking to relational sociology for theoretical insights about education across a variety of contexts (see Kolluri & Tierney in this volume for an extensive discussion).

Applying insights from relational sociology in education research has primarily come in the form of social network analysis (Daly 2010). Social network analysis (SNA) refers to a family of theories and methods that seek to formally measure the positions and structures of networks, how such configurations emerge, and the extent to which they influence access to material and nonmaterial resources (Borgatti, Everett, & Johnson 2013; Wasserman & Faust 1994). To date, education researchers have used SNA to examine a wide variety of topics and, in the process, have illustrated how an emphasis on social relations can inform theory, practice, and policy in educational contexts (see Kalamkarian et al. and McCabe in this volume for examples).

Although the use of SNA in education research continues to grow, this approach is just one of many possible tools that make use of intuitions from relational sociology. In this essay, I draw from recent advances in field theory to argue for a broader understanding of relational approaches to education research. In particular, I maintain that it is necessary to embed networks within the social arenas (i.e., fields) that define the rules, conflicts, and boundaries within and through which actors strive to acquire resources. In addition, I extend the emphasis on relational structures such as networks and fields to concepts that define the experiential and contingent aspects of these structures from the perspective of actors. Taken together, this approach to relational analysis maintains an inherent interest in dynamic relations over fixed attributes while offering potential insights that network concepts alone are not always equipped to provide.

Following the theoretical argument just outlined, I discuss a set of empirical considerations ranging from the development of a research agenda to issues concerning methodology and practical application. Studies that draw on relational theories and methods are often messier and less outcome-oriented than more traditional variable-based approaches to research, and this can make it difficult for researchers to translate their work into tangible recommendations. This consideration is especially relevant for education researchers whose work is increasingly expected to directly inform policy and practice.

Relational Sociology: From Attributes to Relations

The perspectives that make up relational sociology are diverse and draw on a wide range of theoretical traditions. Nevertheless, these perspectives share the assumption that dynamic relationships are the fundamental units of social reality (Emirbayer 1997). That is, the aspects of our lives that are deemed "social" derive meaning through relationships that are in a constant state of motion and negotiation across time and space (Abbott 1997). This understanding of social reality is accompanied by a corresponding set of assumptions about how such relationships can be understood in practical and theoretical terms. Indeed, relational sociologists have been relentlessly concerned with developing methodological tools that adequately simulate the relationships that serve as the foundation of all social phenomena (Abbott 2004; Bourdieu, Passeron, & Chamboredon 1991).

That social life is made up of dynamic relationships likely presents as a redundant statement to virtually any sociologist (and most social scientists in general) regardless of their sympathies toward explicitly relational theories. The divergence of relational sociology appears not through this basic assumption but in how researchers interpret it through their work. In the field of sociology of education, for example, the dominant approach to examining educational questions is rooted in the status attainment model of social mobility and stratification (Kerckhoff 1976; Sewell, Haller, & Ohlendorf 1970; Warren & Hauser 1997). To be sure, this model depicts educational outcomes as a dynamic interplay between ascribed (e.g., family income) and achieved (e.g., academic performance) characteristics. However, these characteristics (or attributes) are assigned (at least implicitly) primary agency in the process of status attainment. Attributes of individuals, such as "ability" and "female," are at the center of social action, and these attributes are assumed to independently influence attainment outcomes. This assumption is on full display in the use of statistical tools that treat the variable attributes of people as having stable and predictable qualities independent of the actors to whom the attributes are associated (Abbott 1988; Lieberson 1985).

The implication of assigning attributes primary agency in social action is that relational qualities such as family income and race are treated as static essences (or substances; see Cassirer 1953) of people and thus as proxies of the social relations in which action is embedded. Yet this does not mean that such models are without merit. To the contrary, arguably the most substantial work on inequality in education has emerged from the status attainment model of social stratification (Schneider 2003). For instance, a long tradition of stratification researchers focusing on the social organization of schooling have compiled mounds of evidence that convincingly illustrates how curricular tracks systematically structure unequal outcomes across socioeconomic and racial categories (e.g., Alexander, Cook, & McDill 1978; Domina & Saldana 2012; Gamoran 1987; Lucas 1999; Lucas & Berends 2002). This body of work has been instrumental in placing social inequality at the center of education policy debates. Nevertheless, while the theoretical assumptions driving this work have illuminated important aspects of inequality in education, the social relationships that create, sustain, and transcend inequality are largely obscured from view (Bourdieu 1998).

SNA and Education

What, then, is a researcher to do if they are primarily concerned with understanding the relational contexts of education beyond simply examining the attributes of actors or organizations? To date, the answer has been SNA, which embodies the core assumptions of relational sociology by emphasizing that the relations between actors serve as the medium through which social action is influenced. Whereas traditional models of academic achievement or degree attainment focus on the attributes of students (e.g., ability, parental education), network models assume that these outcomes are influenced through the structure of relations in which students are embedded (i.e., their networks). Such relations can vary widely, including interactions (e.g., seeks advice from), flows (e.g., acquires information from), or kinship (e.g., sibling of) (Borgatti & Ofem 2010). Attributes remain an important component of SNA but take on a decidedly different role in theory and analysis. For example, network researchers have found that actors tend to form ties with those sharing similar attributes (i.e., homophily; see McPherson, Smith-Lovin, & Cook 2001). In addition, network analysts conceptualize attributes in terms of relationships between actors (e.g., "same gender as") rather than as qualities of individuals (e.g., "female").

The proliferation of SNA in education has occurred alongside similar developments in other applied fields (e.g., health; see Valente 2010). Much of the work thus far has been concentrated in the literature on teachers, school leaders, and reform implementation at the K–12 level (e.g., Coburn & Russell 2008; Daly 2010; Daly & Finnigan 2011; Daly, Moolenaar, Bolivar, & Burke 2010; Jabbar 2015; Keuning, Van Geel, Visscher, Fox, & Moolenaar 2016; Penuel, Riel, Krause, & Frank 2009; Siciliano 2016). One of the central insights emerging from this work is that despite the bureaucratic structure of the education system, informal social networks have a profound impact on educational change—whether at the level of practice or policy. As a result, scholars working in this area of the literature argue that network theory is not simply a tool to understand policy and practice, it is also the theory of action that should drive educational change (Daly & Finnigan 2010).

In addition to the work on reform implementation, two other areas of the education literature have seen an increase in the use of SNA. First, researchers focusing on postsecondary education are turning to SNA to investigate the network context of student persistence and degree completion (e.g., Biancani & McFarland 2013; Chambliss & Takacs 2014; Grunspan, Wiggins, & Goodreau 2014; McCabe 2016; Rios-Aguilar & Deil-Amen 2012; Thomas 2000). This work is a logical expansion of the popular social integration model of postsecondary persistence and departure (Braxton, Shaw Sullivan, & Johnson 1997; Tinto 1975). Second, scholars interested in policy change across all levels of the education system have begun using SNA to describe how networks of foundations and intermediary organizations are transforming the education policy landscape (Au & Ferrare 2014, 2015; Ball & Junemann 2012; Ferrare & Reynolds 2016; Ferrare & Setari 2018; Kretchmar, Sondel, & Ferrare 2014, 2016; Reckhow, 2012; Reckhow & Snyder 2014; Scott, 2015; Scott & Jabbar 2014). Taken together, these areas of the literature have helped add new insights to old questions and adapted to the changing contexts of educational practice and policy.

Although SNA has been the most important medium through which insights from relational sociology have influenced education research, it has largely overshadowed the broader set of conceptual developments emerging from this tradition. In particular, advances in field theory have provided a foundation for extending relational insights beyond the observable network of ties in which actors are embedded (Fligstein & McAdam 2012), as well as the aesthetic experiences of social life (Martin 2011) and the system of meanings that emerge through relational social structures (Mohr 2013). That is, alongside the task of embedding actors within the structure of relations that constitute the contexts of their actions, relational scholars have pushed for a deeper understanding of how actors perceive constraints and affordances in the qualities of these contexts. In this sense, just as it is necessary to embed actors in structures of relations, a more expansive relational project involves simultaneously examining those relations within the realm of individual and group experience. Building on this existing body of work, I argue that this is best accomplished through a field-theoretical framework that encompasses and extends beyond network concepts.

Embedding Networks in Fields

Relational sociologists have long maintained an interest in the relationship between mental structures and social structures. In an insightful work of intellectual history, Mische (2011) points out that significant advancements in relational sociology occurred in the mid-1990s when a group of scholars from interpretive and positivist orientations converged at a number of New York City–based universities. During this time, well-known scholars such as Charles Tilly and Harrison White were pushed to adapt their theories to account for the role of language, identity, and meaning making while emerging interpretive scholars were considering how cultural analysis might benefit from the insights derived from the SNA literature (see, e.g., Emirbayer & Goodwin 1994). In the years that followed, scholars continued to advance theoretical perspectives that accounted for the dynamic interplay between social networks and culture (DiMaggio 2011; Mische, Diani, & McAdam 2003; Mohr & Rawlings 2012). Appropriately, then, some of the most important advances in relational sociology emerged through a set of interactions that closely simulated the theoretical assumptions that were simultaneously under construction.

During a similar timeframe, Bourdieu was arguing that social and mental structures are intricately tied through a dialectical relationship in which objective social divisions between actors correspond to the subjective "principles of vision and division" through which actors experience these boundaries (see, e.g., Bourdieu 1984, 1995, 1996). The "objective social divisions" to which Bourdieu was referring are properties of social fields, understood as "structured spaces of positions (or posts) whose properties depend on their position within these spaces and which can be analyzed independently of the characteristics of their occupants (which are partly determined by them)" (Bourdieu 1993, 72). Meanwhile, Bourdieu understood the "subjective principles of vision and division" through the concept of *habitus*—the set of dispositions through which actors interpret and anticipate possible actions from the point of view of their position in social fields.

The relational point of view in Bourdieu's field theory is relentless. Fields are structured spaces of social relations, made up of positions that derive their properties in relation to other positions from which actors make sense of the world. Sense making is also understood relationally as both a product shaped by the accumulated conflicts and boundaries of fields and a structuring force that gives form to these divisions. This relational view of relations led to Bourdieu's skepticism toward SNA:

> The task of science is to uncover the structure of the distribution of species of capital which tends to determine the structure of individual or collective stances taken, through the interests and dispositions it conditions. In network analysis, the study of

these underlying structures has been sacrificed to the analysis of the particular linkages . . . and flows . . . through which they become visible. (Bourdieu & Wacquant 1992, 114)

Thus, for Bourdieu, it was not enough to examine the structure of network ties or even the role of culture within this context. Rather, the project of relational sociology, he argued, is to identify the underlying rules and resources that structure the social arenas (i.e., fields) that encompass network ties and cultural practices.

Ties to Positions

Bourdieu's critical view of networks was rooted in a broader concern for identifying structures of domination and symbolic violence that are not always immediately visible through observable network ties. Yet his dismissal of SNA as a viable tool for relational analysis was misguided (Mohr 2013)—especially toward the efforts of fostering a relational sociology of education. Indeed, networks are crucial to such a project because they are the medium through which educational actors (students, teachers, policy makers, etc.) traverse between and maintain boundaries around positions in social fields. In this sense, networks constitute ties between actors and positions. Embedding networks in fields is thus a process of situating ties between actors within a broader (and admittedly more abstract) set of relations structured by the rules, boundaries, and resources that define a given social space. However, this does not mean that network ties are simply a reflection of some invisible social force. Rather, ties and positions are coconstitutive and must be considered as interdependent sets of social relations.

In a typical Bourdieuian field analysis, actors are positioned in a multidimensional space structured by the volume, composition, and temporal trajectory of capital germane to the field (Bourdieu 1984). The volume of capital simply refers to the total amount of resources available to an actor in a given social arena, and the composition speaks to the specific type(s) of resources that make up the total volume (e.g., scientific prestige versus administrative power in the academic field; see Bourdieu 1988). The qualities of positions are established relationally vis-à-vis other positions in the field (Bourdieu 1993). This means that field positions are interdependent even when separated by great distances (i.e., volume and composition of capital). However, networks play a crucial role in these spaces because they link and separate actors within and between positions. For example, when actor *i* in position *K* establishes a tie to actor *j* in position *L* (see figure 2.1), the tie links not only actors but also the broader contexts (i.e., positions) in which they are situated. These ties then serve as a medium through which material and nonmaterial resources can be transferred across field positions.

Conceptualizing the embeddedness of networks in this way contextualizes both networks and fields. The absence of ties across positions, for instance, reinforces boundaries between positions and serves as a potential site of conflict over resources. Meanwhile, the presence of network ties across positions can expose these boundaries and instigate or mitigate conflicts within fields. These processes are precisely what drive both stability and change in social fields (Fligstein & McAdam 2012). The tie between actors *i* and *j*—and subsequently the affiliation between positions

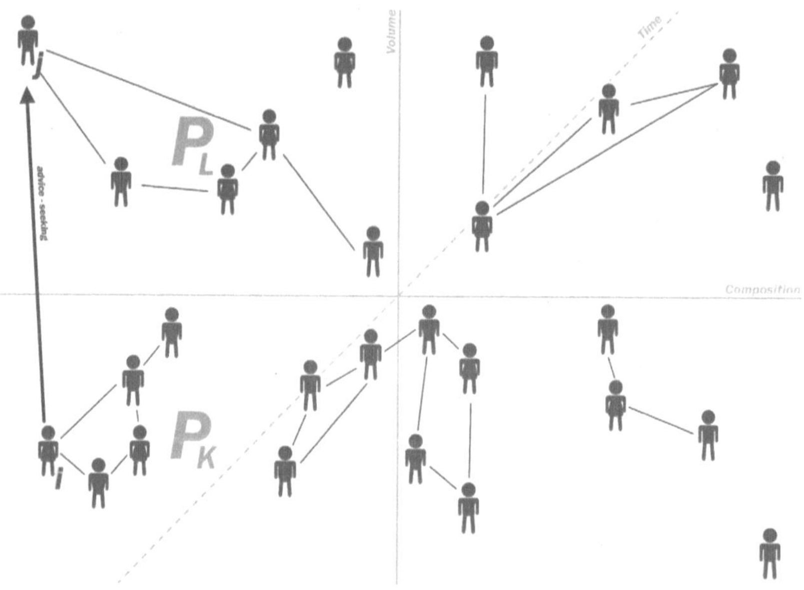

Figure 2.1. Hypothetical advice-seeking tie, $i \rightarrow j$, across positions, $P_K \rightarrow P_L$, embedded in a Bourdieuian field space. Volume refers to the total amount of field-relevant capital that defines a given position and composition refers to the specific types of capital that make up the total volume. Source: Joseph Ferrare.

K and *L*—introduce the potential to challenge or reinforce boundaries. This is especially important in education fields, which serve as sites of social reproduction and mobility.

A hypothetical example is warranted. Imagine that actor *i* in figure 2.1 is a first-generation college-going student majoring in psychology and person *j* is a tenured professor of psychology at a university. Each actor is embedded in a network(s) at the same time they are situated in a position within the field of higher education. As indicated, these positions are determined by the total amount (i.e., volume) and type(s) of field-relevant capital that each actor possesses vis-à-vis others. If student *i* enters into an advice-seeking relationship with professor *j*, this provides *i* with access to potentially valuable resources (i.e., the professor's social or scientific capital) and serves as a passage for each actor to "travel" to another region of a social field and experience the meaning systems and identities through which actors in those regions define the field and its rules. There is, then, a duality of influence between networks and fields. That is, although the underlying structure of a social field shapes the formation of ties (e.g., first-generation students may be uncomfortable establishing a connection with a professor), once established, such ties may exert a force of change on the field (e.g., the student experiences social mobility or the professor changes her practice to be more responsive to other first-generation students).

The primary advantage of embedding networks in fields is that it pushes scholars to look for multiple layers of relations—both observable ties and affiliations as well as latent social positions. I have argued that embedding networks in fields illuminates the underlying structure of social space that shapes and is shaped by the ties between actors. Ties between actors create affiliations between positions, which can reinforce or disturb the rules and conflicts governing the distribution of capital structuring a given field of action. Whereas network theory tends to conceptualize influence locally (i.e., through direct or indirect ties), field theory allows for influence at a distance even in the absence of an observable network path. But there remains another important component to this story concerning the ways actors perceive and experience constraints and affordances in networks and the broader fields in which they are situated. An adequate accounting of this process necessitates a view of the individual level from the perspective of first-person experience, a view that sociologists of education often neglect.

Positions and Perceptions

Thus far, I have conceptualized multiple layers of social relations that shape action locally and at a distance. By itself, though, this perspective presents action as largely determined by exogenous "forces," which in effect means that the actor's affective relationship to the structural environment is assumed to be of little importance. Such a view misses out on a crucial component of action (Sayer 2011). Consider the following scenario. I recently considered proposing a new undergraduate program at my university. As I sought advice from colleagues, I was struck by the amount of red tape I would have go through to turn this idea into a reality. I also perceived this work as a form of service that could potentially distract from research and teaching—the tasks that define whether I will be granted tenure. Soon enough, I had dropped the idea entirely. The set of relationships that constitute the governance structure of my university had exerted an exogenous influence on my action. However, my department chair was not so easily defeated. She is not naive to the red tape, of course. Rather, her position is endowed with a greater composition of administrative capital, which helped her view university governance as an opportunity where I saw constraint. Furthermore, what I conceptualized as the distraction of service could be viewed as an administrative opportunity for someone in this position. After a conversation with my chair, whom I have grown to trust, I (skeptically) agreed that it might be worth a try.

This example illustrates that the task of embedding networks in fields also requires that we link these interdependent social relations to the perceptions that shape how actors interpret trajectories of action. As noted, Bourdieu was deeply concerned with this relationship. However, he often conceptualized actors' mental structures as mere reflections of positions in social fields (Bourdieu 1990). More recently, relational sociologists working to build on Bourdieu's field theory have sought to clarify this assumption. In particular, Martin (2003, 2011) has argued that actors directly perceive possibilities and constraints in social relations, and that these perceptions are contingent on how actors are positioned in the situation. To make his case, Martin builds from early work in field theory that had advanced relational understandings of individual perception (see also Mohr 2013). This work was initially undertaken by Gestalt psychologists (Koffka 1935; Kohler 1947; Wertheimer 1944) and later expanded by social-psychologist Kurt Lewin (1951).

Martin's engagement with social-psychological field theory focused primarily on the concepts of valence (Lewin 1951) and affordance (Gibson 1986), or what Gestalt psychologists referred to as the "demand character" of objects in an actor's environment. Objects contain information that is interpreted by actors as either enabling or constraining certain actions. For instance, a tree affords a shady spot to sit on a hot summer day and is thus experienced as having a positive valence. One of Martin's (2011) key contributions has been to extend the concepts of valence and affordance in objects in the environment to positions in social fields. Positions, he argues, contain information about possible action trajectories through social space (see also Ferrare & Apple 2015). In effect, this information serves as a set of instructions, albeit with a contingent range of outcomes (see Hutchins 1995). Recall that, as an assistant professor with limited administrative capital, my read of university governance compelled me to retreat from the idea of creating a new program and to resume research activities—an action trajectory more appropriate to the position. In short, my social position served as a heuristic for action (Martin 2011). However, the social tie I have to my department chair offered a glimpse into the information set contained in her position (i.e., a more favorable read of university governance and administrative power). Thus, network ties across field positions—and perceptions of affordances in both sets of relations—coconstituted action in this scenario. This is, in essence, what it means to embed networks in fields.

Empirical Considerations

To this point, I have tried to articulate an expanded model of relational sociology for education research, one that incorporates the insights of SNA into a field theory of action attentive to the structure and experience of social life. Admittedly, the expanded model offered above introduces a great deal of complexity into relational analysis. In particular, the model calls attention to three interrelated sets of relations through which researchers can interpret and explain practices and policies in education: (1) observable networks; (2) the set of rules, resources, and boundaries that structure network activity (i.e., fields); and (3) the constraints and affordances actors experience in these social relations. Although it will not always be feasible (or necessary) to simultaneously address all three components, ongoing developments in research design and analytic techniques are making this integrative task increasingly accessible. In this section, my objective is to identify the areas of the literature most amenable to this framework, as well as identify methodological tools that researchers can use to address empirical questions.

Even though educational practices and policy making are relational activities by definition, there are specific segments of the literature in which this framework can be most relevant. The first is in the area of studies dealing with the role of education in social mobility and stratification. This body of work is primarily concerned with identifying the structures through which students' motivations and abilities interact with their family backgrounds and ascribed identities in ways that enable and constrain educational attainment. As noted, much of this work is grounded in the status attainment model (Kerckhoff 1976; Sewell et al. 1970; Warren & Hauser 1997). Although the work that has emerged through this tradition has been very successful at identifying social mobility and stratification, the practices by which these outcomes arise have seen less attention.

Recent ethnographic work has begun to fill in these gaps, especially as it relates to the role of social class in shaping advantages and disadvantages across the K–16 levels (e.g., Armstrong & Hamilton 2013; Calarco 2014a, 2014b; Lareau 2000, 2002; Weis, Cipollone, & Jenkins 2014). These works offer excellent examples of integrating two of the three components to the model outlined above. In *Paying for the Party*, for example, Armstrong and Hamilton (2013) identify the rules, boundaries, and resources that differentially structure opportunities among a cohort of women at a flagship research university. They provide powerful narratives of how students directly experience constraints and affordances in these opportunity structures in ways that reproduce social inequality. While work like this must continue, it is also important to understand how some students manage to transcend social class positions across generations. Integrating formal SNA into this work may facilitate such insights, as this form of social mobility necessitates the formation of ties across disparate positions in social space. Thus, a perspective that embeds networks in fields is well adapted to unpack the moving parts of these processes.

The social organization of schools and universities is another area of research for which this perspective is well suited. Educational organizations are bounded structures characterized by formal and informal positions. Not surprisingly, then, relational sociologists of education have had the greatest impact thus far in this area of the literature. In particular, researchers have used network and field theory to examine social positions that emerge through students' course-taking patterns at the secondary level (Ferrare 2013; Frank, Muller, & Schiller 2008; Friedkin & Thomas 1997) and persistence and degree-seeking patterns at the postsecondary level (Bourdieu 1996; McCabe 2016; Rawlings & Bourgeois 2004). These works offer an example of new insights that relational perspectives can contribute to long-standing questions of interest in education. Most notably, McCabe's (2016) analysis in *Connecting in College* illustrates the processes by which students form social networks in college settings, including an in-depth look at how they perceive possibilities in the structure of their networks. Future studies can build on these insights by situating the latter processes within the broader set of organizational rules, boundaries, and resources that support and interfere with the types of network formation that lead to academic and professional success.

A field-theoretical perspective as outlined above may open up new understandings concerning persistent patterns of gender segregation in academic and occupational trajectories (Mann & DiPrete 2013; Morgan, Gelbgiser, & Weeden 2013). For example, recent evidence from psychology suggests that gender disparities in the sciences are shaped by the interplay of distal (i.e., broad contexts) and proximal (i.e., attitudes and perceived strengths) factors (Stoet & Geary 2018). Field theory anticipates that the latter perceptions are formed in relation to the information embedded in academic fields of study. That is, gender is an individual identity and one that is situated in the system of tacit rules, boundaries, and resources that structure institutions and organizations. Future work should examine whether certain types of social networks are able to mediate the ways actors perceive gender-appropriate roles and positions. Recent evidence in organizational studies suggests that this may be productive line of work in educational settings (Brands & Mehra 2018).

Finally, the politics of education reform and policy change is a broad area of the literature where a field theory of educational action can have immediate impact. Whether one is examining local reforms (e.g., school closures), state-level policies (e.g., school choice), or nationwide trends (e.g., competency-based education), such analyses involve identifying coalitions (i.e., networks and positions) of actors and the rules and resources shaping the collective struggles and competitions germane to the policy subsystem (i.e., field). This perspective has gained momentum in recent years, as policy network analysis (Rhodes 2006) from political science has taken hold in education policy studies (Au & Ferrare 2015;

Ball & Junemann 2012; Reckhow 2012). Whereas traditional models of policy change emphasize vested interests and incremental changes (e.g., punctuated equilibrium; see Baumgartner & Jones 1993), policy scholars are increasingly pointing to the crucial role of networks in illuminating these processes—especially in the context of market-based reforms that traverse the public and private spheres. However, this body of work has yet to fully embed these networks within the broader strategic action fields that influence policy network formation and change (Fligstein & McAdam 2011, 2012). In an era of education policy defined by shifting alliances and dramatic transformation (Galey 2015), field theory is likely to offer a powerful tool to anticipate these changes and identify possible coalitions that can foster durable policy changes.

Methods for Relational Analysis

If the theoretical framework of embedding networks in fields is complex, it is reasonable to expect the task of empirically capturing these constellations of relations to be out of reach. Relational sociologists have generally been critical of the familiar tools in the sociologist's toolkit (most notably general linear models; see Abbott 1988), and have instead sought to identify techniques that have internal logics consistent with relational theories (Abbott 2004; Ferrare 2009). This is especially true among those working within a field-theoretical framework. A key challenge for this body of work is that relational methods such as SNA are often excluded from graduate training programs. However, the growing popularity of SNA in education (including dedicated textbooks; see Carolan 2014) provides the potential to build a broader tradition of relational analysis in education and the social sciences more generally. In addition to SNA, relational sociologists have been hard at work developing new techniques to measure field effects, such as case-based regression analysis (Breiger & Melamed 2014) and spatial models of fields (Martin, Slez, & Borkenhagen 2016).

The perspective outlined in this chapter requires tools that identify not only structural patterns of fields and networks but also the aesthetic qualities of these spaces as experienced by actors. In this regard, recent advances in relational ethnography can be especially helpful. Desmond (2014), for example, distinguishes relational ethnography from traditional forms of ethnographic work in multiple ways. Most notably, he argues that relational theorists should emphasize fields, boundaries, processes, and conflicts over places, bounded groups, processed people, and shared group cultures (see chapters by Tichavakunda and Lanford in this volume). This approach to ethnography builds on the Bourdieuian tradition (1979, 1990; Bourdieu et al. 1991) of constructing the object(s) of research as relational processes rather than fixed qualities and substances (see also Mische 2008).

There are some available strategies specifically attuned to simultaneously embedding actors' networks in fields in relation to their perceptions of constraints and affordances in these structures. For example, combining SNA, case-based (or Q-mode; see Bartholomew, Steele, Moustaki, & Galbraith 2008) clustering or scaling methods, and concept coding of qualitative data (e.g., interview transcripts, archival documents) offers a parsimonious illustration of a complex, multidimensional data space. Suppose, for example, researchers have collected academic advice-seeking network data among students at a university in an effort to better understand how they persist in their academic objectives. Typically, researchers would calculate a range of measures related to the structure (e.g., density, effective size) and composition (e.g., homophily) of these networks. Field theorists can take this $n \times m$ (students by network measures) matrix and use clustering techniques (Everitt, Landau, Leese, & Stahl 2011) to partition students into groups based on the degree to which they share network characteristics. In fact, there are a wide range of strategies in SNA that produce similar outcomes, such as block modeling and equivalence (for an introduction, see Borgatti et al. 2013). These techniques can reduce the data space from a set of individual actors and their personal networks to a set of latent groups sharing ties to similar field positions (see Faust 1988).

With the network measures transformed into a set of positions, the next step involves accounting for the constraints and affordances that our hypothetical students experience through their positions in relation to their academic objectives. For this purpose, relational researchers can conduct interviews with participating students and code the transcripts using any number of coding strategies (see, e.g., Corbin & Strauss 2008; Glaser & Strauss 1967; Saldana 2013). Once coded, the data can be embedded into the structure of relations toward which they are directed through any number of scaling approaches, such as multidimensional scaling (Borg & Groenen 2005; Kruskal & Wish 1978) or correspondence analysis (Greenacre 2007). Multidimensional scaling and correspondence analysis are similar to cluster analysis, only instead of partitioning objects into mutually exclusive groups, these techniques represent differences between objects as distances in a two-dimensional space. For example,

Ferrare (2013) used multidimensional scaling and correspondence analysis to analyze the latent course-taking patterns associated with various postsecondary trajectories (for additional examples of these techniques, see Ferrare & Hora 2014; Rawlings & Bourgeois 2004). When applied to interview data, one can plot the emergent themes in relation to the clusters of network qualities as described above. The resulting plot would offer a full representation of the relational structures and perceptions through which students navigate and interpret possible actions as they pursue their academic objectives.

There are, then, a wide variety of methodological tools available to those seeking to undertake relational projects in education. As noted already, one challenge is that these techniques are (at least perceived as) less accessible than more traditional approaches to social science research. Another obstacle concerns how relational theories and methods can have a direct influence on policy and practice. This is especially important in education research given the strong association to practitioners in schools, universities, and policy-making institutions. Relational scholarship typically eschews designs that predict outcomes such as test score growth or degree attainment. Increasingly, such questions are the exclusive domain of experimental and quasi-experimental designs (Murnane & Willett 2011). Although it may be fruitful to consider how relational approaches can illuminate these outcome-based questions, I argue that it is at least as important to consider alternative models of work relevant to the public sphere beyond academia. Recent examples of these alternatives using relational techniques to tell first-person stories of inequality are available (Bourdieu 2006; Desmond 2016), but these should not be considered exhaustive. Just as relational sociology reflects a departure from traditional conceptions of the social world, the vision of how this work can influence the public sphere must be at least as radical.

Conclusion

The primary objective of this chapter was to establish a foundation for unifying multiple relational concepts into a single framework based in a field theory of educational action. In particular, I argued that networks should be situated within the social arenas that define the rules, boundaries, and conflicts around which educational actors struggle for resources. In the process, following recent work in relational sociology, I pushed this structural argument into the terrain of individual perception and experience. I then highlighted some areas of the literature where this framework may offer the potential to illuminate new insights and introduced some analytical techniques that extend beyond the current emphasis on SNA. Moving forward, the framework offered in this chapter—and others grounded in relational sociological theory—needs to be further developed and revised through rigorous empirical studies that integrate a wide variety of data and analytical tools. I have merely scratched the surface of the theoretical, methodological, and communicative work needed to push this perspective into the center of educational research agendas.

References

Abbott, A. (1988). Transcending general linear reality. *Sociological Theory, 6*(2), 169–86.

Abbott, A. (1997). Of time and space: The contemporary relevance of the Chicago School. *Social Forces, 75*(4), 1149–82.

Abbott, A. (2004). *Methods of discovery: Heuristics for the social sciences.* New York, NY: W. W. Norton.

Alexander, K. L., Cook, M., & McDill, E. L. (1978). Curriculum tracking and educational stratification: Some further evidence. *American Sociological Review, 43*(1), 47–66.

Armstrong, E. A., & Hamilton, L. T. (2013). *Paying for the party: How college maintains inequality.* Cambridge, MA: Harvard University Press.

Au, W., & Ferrare, J. J. (2014). Sponsors of policy: A network analysis of wealthy elites, their affiliated philanthropies, and charter school reform in Washington State. *Teachers College Record, 116*(11), http://www.tcrecord.org, ID 17387.

Au, W., & Ferrare, J. J. (Eds.). (2015). *Mapping corporate education reform: Power and policy networks in the neoliberal state.* New York, NY: Routledge.

Ball, S. J., & Junemann, C. (2012). *Networks, new governance and education.* Bristol, UK: Policy Press.

Bartholomew, D. J., Steele, F., Moustaki, I., & Galbraith, J. (2008). *Analysis of multivariate social science data* (2nd ed.). Boca Raton, FL: Chapman & Hall/CRC.

Baumgartner, F., & Jones, B. D. (1993). *Agendas and instability in American politics.* Chicago, IL: University of Chicago Press.

Biancani, S., & McFarland, D. A. (2013). Social networks research in higher education. In *Higher education: Handbook of theory and research*, edited by Michael B. Paulsen, vol. 28, 151–215. Dordrecht, Netherlands: Springer.

Borg, I., & Groenen, P. J. F. (2005). *Modern multidimensional scaling: Theory and applications.* New York, NY: Springer.

Borgatti, S. P., Everett, M. G., & Johnson, J. C. (2013). *Analyzing social networks*. London, UK: Sage.

Borgatti, S. P., & Ofem, B. (2010). Overview: Social network thoery and analysis. In *Social network theory and educational change*, edited by A. J. Daly, 17–29. Cambridge, MA: Harvard Education Press.

Bourdieu, P. (1979). *Algeria 1960*. Cambridge, UK: Cambridge University Press.

Bourdieu, P. (1984). *Distinction: A social critique of the judgment of taste*, translated by R. Nice. Cambridge, MA: Routledge & Kegan Paul.

Bourdieu, P. (1988). *Homo academicus*. Stanford, CA: Stanford University Press.

Bourdieu, P. (1990). *The logic of practice*. Stanford, CA: Stanford University Press.

Bourdieu, P. (1993). *Sociology in question*. London, UK: Sage.

Bourdieu, P. (1995). *The rules of art: The genesis and structure of the literary field*, translated by S. Emanuel. Stanford, CA: Stanford University Press.

Bourdieu, P. (1996). *The state nobility: Elite schools in the field of power*. Cambridge, UK: Polity Press.

Bourdieu, P. (1998). *Practical reason: On the theory of action*. Stanford, CA: Stanford University Press.

Bourdieu, P. (2006). *The weight of the world: Social suffering in contemporary society* (3rd ed.). Oxford, UK: Blackwell.

Bourdieu, P., Passeron, J.-C., & Chamboredon, J.-C. (1991). *The craft of sociology: Epistemological preliminaries*. New York, NY: Walter de Gruyter.

Bourdieu, P., & Wacquant, L. J. D. (1992). *An invitation to reflexive sociology*. Chicago, IL: University of Chicago Press.

Brands, R., & Mehra, A. (2018). Gender, brokerage, and performance: A construal approach. *Academy of Management Journal*, https://doi.org/10.5465/amj.2016.0860.

Braxton, J. M., Shaw Sullivan, A. V., & Johnson, R. M. Jr. (1997). Appraising Tinto's theory of college student departure. In *Higher education: Handbook of theory and research*, edited by J. C. Smart, 107–64. New York, NY: Agathon.

Breiger, R. L., & Melamed, D. (2014). The duality of organizations and their attributes: Turning regression modeling "inside out." In *Contemporary perspectives on organizational social networks*, edited by D. J. Brass, G. Labianca, A. Mehra, D. S. Halgin, & S. P. Borgatti, vol. 40, 263–75. Bingley, UK: Emerald Group.

Calarco, J. M. (2014a). Coached for the classroom: Parents' cultural transmission and children's reproduction of educational inequalities. *American Sociological Review*, *79*(5), 1015–37.

Calarco, J. M. (2014b). The inconsistent curriculum: Cultural tool kits and student interpretations of ambiguous expectations. *Social Psychology Quarterly*, *77*(2), 185–209.

Carolan, B. V. (2014). *Social network analysis and education: Theory, methods and applications*. Thousand Oaks, CA: Sage.

Cassirer, E. (1953). *Substance and function*. New York, NY: Dover.

Chambliss, D. F., & Takacs, C. G. (2014). *How college works*. Cambridge, MA: Harvard University Press.

Coburn, C. E., & Russell, J. L. (2008). District policy and teachers' social networks. *Educational Evaluation and Policy Analysis, 30*(3), 203–35.

Corbin, J., & Strauss, A. L. (2008). *Basics of qualitative research* (3rd ed.). Thousand Oaks, CA: Sage.

Daly, A. J. (Ed.). (2010). *Social network theory and educational change*. Cambridge, MA: Harvard University Press.

Daly, A. J., & Finnigan, K. S. (2010). A bridge between worlds: Understanding network structure to understand change strategy. *Journal of Educational Change, 11*(2), 111–38.

Daly, A. J., & Finnigan, K. (2011). The ebb and flow of social network ties between district leaders under high-stakes accountability. *American Educational Research Journal, 48*(1), 39–79.

Daly, A. J., Moolenaar, N. M., Bolivar, J. M., & Burke, P. (2010). Relationships in reform: The role of teachers' social networks. *Journal of Educational Administration, 48*(3), 359–91.

Desmond, M. (2014). Relational ethnography. *Theory and Society, 43*(1), 547–79.

Desmond, M. (2016). *Evicted: Poverty and profit in the American city*. New York, NY: Broadway Books.

DiMaggio, P. (2011). Cultural networks. In *The SAGE handbook of social network analysis*, edited by J. Scott & P. J. Carrington, 286–300. Thousand Oaks, CA: Sage.

Domina, T., & Saldana, J. (2012). Does raising the bar level the playing field? Mathematics curricular intensification and inequality in American high schools, 1982–2004. *American Educational Research Journal, 49*(4), 685–708.

Emirbayer, M. (1997). Manifesto for a relational sociology. *American Journal of Sociology, 103*(2), 281–317.

Emirbayer, M., & Goodwin, J. (1994). Network analysis, culture, and the problem of agency. *American Journal of Sociology, 99*, 1411–54.

Everitt, B. S., Landau, S., Leese, M., & Stahl, D. (2011). *Cluster analysis* (5th ed.). West Sussex, UK: John Wiley & Sons.

Faust, K. (1988). Comparison of methods for positional analysis: Structural and general equivalences. *Social Networks, 10*, 313–41.

Ferrare, J. J. (2009). Can critical education research be "quantitative"? In *Routledge international handbook of critical education*, edited by M. W. Apple, W. Au, & L. Gandin, 465–81. New York, NY: Routledge.

Ferrare, J. J. (2013). The duality of courses and students: A field-theoretic analysis of secondary school course-taking. *Sociology of Education, 86*(2), 139–57.

Ferrare, J. J., & Apple, M. W. (2015). Field theory and educational practice: Bourdieu and the didactic qualities of local field positions in educational contexts. *Cambridge Journal of Education, 45*(1), 43–59.

Ferrare, J. J., & Hora, M. T. (2014). Cultural models of teaching and learning: Challenges and opportunities for undergraduate math and science education. *Journal of Higher Education, 85*(6), 792–825.

Ferrare, J. J., & Reynolds, K. (2016). Has the elite foundation agenda spread beyond the gates? An organizational network analysis of non-major philanthropic giving in K12 education. *American Journal of Education, 123*(1), 137–69.

Ferrare, J. J., & Setari, R. R. (2018). Converging on choice: The interstate flow of foundation dollars to charter school organizations. *Educational Researcher, 47*(1), 34–45.

Fligstein, N., & McAdam, D. (2011). Toward a general theory of strategic action fields. *Sociological Theory, 29*(1), 1–26.

Fligstein, N., & McAdam, D. (2012). *A theory of fields*. Oxford, UK: Oxford University Press.

Frank, K. A., Muller, C., & Schiller, K. (2008). The social dynamics of mathematics coursetaking in high school. *American Journal of Sociology, 113*, 1645–96.

Friedkin, N. E., & Thomas, S. L. (1997). Social positions in schooling. *Sociology of Education, 70*(4), 239–55.

Galey, S. (2015). Education politics and policy: Emerging institutions, interests, and ideas. *Policy Studies Journal, 43*(S1), S12–39.

Gamoran, A. (1987). The stratification of high school learning opportunities. *Sociology of Education, 60*, 135–55.

Gibson, J. J. (1986). *The ecological approach to visual perception*. Princeton, NJ: Princeton University Press.

Glaser, B. G., & Strauss, A. L. (1967). *The discovery of grounded theory: Strategies for qualitative research*. Chicago, IL: Aldine.

Greenacre, M. (2007). *Correspondence analysis in practice* (2nd ed.). Boca Raton, FL: Chapman & Hall/CRC.

Grunspan, D. Z., Wiggins, B. L., & Goodreau, S. M. (2014). Understanding classrooms through social network anlaysis in education research. *CBE-Life Sciences Education, 13*(1), 167–78.

Hutchins, E. (1995). *Cognition in the wild*. Cambridge, MA: MIT Press.

Jabbar, H. (2015). Competitive networks and school leaders' perceptions: The formation of an education marketplace in post-Katrina New Orleans. *American Educational Research Journal, 52*(6), 1093–131.

Kerckhoff, A. C. (1976). The status attainment process: Socialization or allocation? *Social Forces, 55*(2), 368–81.

Keuning, T., Van Geel, M., Visscher, A., Fox, J., & Moolenaar, N. M. (2016). The transformation of schools' social networks during a data-based decision making reform. *Teachers College Record, 118*(1), 1–33.

Koffka, K. (1935). *Principles of gestalt psychology*. New York, NY: Harcourt, Brace & World.

Kohler, W. (1947). *Gestalt psychology: An introduction to new concepts in modern psychology*. New York, NY: Liveright.

Kretchmar, K., Sondel, B., & Ferrare, J. J. (2014). Mapping the terrain: Teach For America, charter school reform, and corporate sponsorship. *Journal of Education Policy, 29*(6), 742–59.

Kretchmar, K., Sondel, B., & Ferrare, J. J. (2016). The power of the network: Teach For America's impact on the deregulation of teacher education. *Educational Policy*, 0895904816637687.

Kruskal, J. B., & Wish, M. (1978). *Multidimensional scaling* (vol. 11). London, UK: Sage.

Lareau, A. (2000). *Home advantage: Social class and parental intervention in elementary education*. Oxford, UK: Rowman & Littlefield.

Lareau, A. (2002). Invisible inequality: Social class and childrearing in black families and white families. *American Sociological Review, 67*(5), 747–76.

Lewin, K. (1951). *Field theory in social science: Selected theoretical papers*. New York, NY: Harper & Row.

Lieberson, S. (1985). *Making it count: The improvement of social research and theory*. Berkeley, CA: University of California Press.

Lucas, S. R. (1999). *Tracking inequality: Stratification and mobility in American high schools*. New York, NY: Teachers College Press.

Lucas, S. R., & Berends, M. (2002). Sociodemographic diversity, correlated achievement, and de facto tracking. *Sociology of Education, 75*(4), 328–48.

Mann, A., & DiPrete, T. A. (2013). Trends in gender segregation in the choice of science and engineering majors. *Social Science Research, 42*, 1519–41.

Martin, J. L. (2003). What is field theory? *American Journal of Sociology, 109*(1), 1–49.

Martin, J. L. (2011). *The explanation of social action*. Oxford, UK: Oxford University Press.

Martin, J. L., Slez, A., & Borkenhagen, C. (2016). Some provisional techniques for quantifying the degree of field effect in social data. *Socius, 2*, 1–18.

McCabe, J. M. (2016). *Connecting in college: How friendship networks matter for academic and social success*. Chicago, IL: University of Chicago Press.

McPherson, M., Smith-Lovin, L., & Cook, J. M. (2001). Birds of a feather: Homophily in social networks. *Annual Review of Sociology, 27*(1), 415–44.

Mische, A. (2008). *Partisan publics: Communication and contention across Brazilian youth activist networks*. Princeton, NJ: Princeton University Press.

Mische, A. (2011). Relational sociology, culture, and agency. In *The SAGE handbook of social network analysis*, edited by John Scott & P. J. Carrington, 80–98. Thousand Oaks, CA: Sage.

Mische, A., Diani, M., & McAdam, D. (2003). Cross-talk in movements: Rethinking the culture-network link. In *Social movements and networks: Relational approaches to collective action*, 258–80. Oxford, UK: Oxford University Press.

Mohr, J. W. (2013). Bourdieu's relational method in theory and practice: From fields and capitals to networks and institutions (and back again). In *Applying relational sociology: Relations, networks, and society*, edited by F. Depelteau & C. Powell, 101–36. New York, NY: Palgrave Macmillan.

Mohr, J. W., & Rawlings, C. (2012). Four ways to measure culture: Social science, hermeneutics, and the cultural turn. In *The Oxford handbood of cultural sociology*, edited by J. C. Alexander, R. Jacobs, & P. Smith, 70–113. Oxford, UK: Oxford University Press.

Morgan, S. L., Gelbgiser, D., & Weeden, K. A. (2013). Feeding the pipeline: Gender, occupational plans, and college major selection. *Social Science Research, 42*(4), 989–1005.

Murnane, R. J., & Willett, J. B. (2011). *Methods matter: Improving causal inference in educational and social science research*. New York, NY: Oxford University Press.

Penuel, W., Riel, M., Krause, A., & Frank, K. A. (2009). Analyzing teachers' professional interactions in a school as social capital: A social network approach. *Teachers College Record, 111*(1), 124–63.

Rawlings, C. M., & Bourgeois, M. D. (2004). The complexity of institutional niches: Credentials and organizational differentiation in a field of U.S. higher education. *Poetics, 32*(6), 411–46.

Reckhow, S. (2012). *Follow the money: How foundation dollars change public school politics*. Oxford, UK: Oxford University Press.

Reckhow, S., & Snyder, J. W. (2014). The expanding role of philanthropy in education politics. *Educational Researcher, 43*(4), 186–95.

Rhodes, R. A. W. (2006). Policy network analysis. In *The Oxford handbook of public policy*, edited by M. Moran, M. Rein, & R. E. Goodin, 425–47. Oxford, UK: Oxford University Press.

Rios-Aguilar, C., & Deil-Amen, R. (2012). Beyond getting in and fitting in: An examination of social networks and professionally relevant social capital among Latina/o university students. *Journal of Hispanic Higher Education, 11*(2), 179–96.

Saldana, J. (2013). *The coding manual for qualitative researchers* (2nd ed.). London: Sage.

Sayer, A. (2011). *Why things matter to people: Social science, values and ethical life*. Cambridge, UK: Cambridge University Press.

Schneider, B. (2003). Sociology of education: An overview of the field at the turn of the twenty-first century. In *Stability and change in American education: Structure, process, and outcomes*, edited by M. T. Hallinan, A. Gamoran, W. Kubitschek, & T. Loveless, 193–226. Clinton Corners, NY: Eliot Werner.

Scott, J. (2015). Foundations and the development of the U.S. charter school policy-planning network: Implications for democratic schooling and civil rights. *Teachers College Record, 117*(14), 131–47.

Scott, J., & Jabbar, H. (2014). The hub and the spokes: Foundations, intermediary organizations, incentivist reforms, and the politics of research evidence. *Educational Policy, 28*(2), 233–57.

Sewell, W. H., Haller, A. O., & Ohlendorf, G. W. (1970). The educational and early occupational status attainment process: Replication and revision. *American Sociological Review, 35*(6), 1014–27.

Siciliano, M. D. (2016). It's the quality not the quantity of ties that matters: Social networks and self-efficacy beliefs. *American Educational Research Journal, 53*(2), 227–62.

Stoet, G., & Geary, D. C. (2018). The gender-equality paradox in science, technology, engineering, and mathematics education. *Psychological Science, OnlineFirst*, 1–13.

Thomas, S. L. (2000). Ties that bind: A social network approach to understanding student integration and persistence. *Journal of Higher Education, 71*(5), 591–615.

Tinto, V. (1975). Dropout from higher education: A theoretical synthesis of recent research. *Review of Educational Research, 45*(1), 89–125.

Valente, T. W. (2010). *Social networks and health: Models, methods, and applications.* Oxford, UK: Oxford University Press.

Warren, J. R., & Hauser, R. M. (1997). Social stratification across three generations: New evidence from the Wisconsin longitudinal study. *American Sociological Review, 62*(4), 561–72.

Wasserman, S., & Faust, K. (1994). *Social network analysis: Methods and applications.* New York, NY: Cambridge University Press.

Weis, L., Cipollone, K., & Jenkins, H. (2014). *Class warfare: Class, race, and college admissions in top-tier secondary schools.* Chicago, IL: University of Chicago Press.

Wertheimer, M. (1944). Gestalt theory. *Social Research, 11*, 78–99.

Chapter 3

Which Truths Shall We Speak to Power?

Relational Sociology in Qualitative Research on Educational Stratification

JULIE R. POSSELT

> If I do not speak in a language that can be understood, there is little possibility of dialogue.
>
> —bell hooks

Education is a powerful field of social reproduction, with the credentials that its institutions award critical for securing further educational, professional, and economic opportunities. Foundations of social inequality today include efforts by elites to use the education system as a means of protecting their status. We see, for example, wealthy parents safeguarding their children's relative standing through childrearing and elementary school choices (Lareau 2011), and through advocacy for their children's academic tracking placements (Lewis & Diamond 2015; Lucas 2001). Institutionalized preferences and practices of well-intended educational professionals also reproduce inequalities, such as those shaping admissions decisions that determine access to selective colleges and graduate programs (Karabel 2005; Milkman, Akinola, & Chugh 2015; Posselt 2016; Stevens 2007). Intentionally or otherwise, educators' unexamined professional practice reproduces systems of stratification as often as it facilitates learning, empowerment, and mobility capable of softening those systems.

As such, and because history provides ample evidence, we cannot rely only on those in positions of power to change schools and schooling. We need change agents positioned inside and outside of educational institutions, who hold more and less social power and professional authority, who have much and little to lose from change. Freire (1993) recognized that even when "members of the oppressor class join the oppressed in their struggle for liberation . . . they must always bring with them the marks of their origin" (60),[1] which may inherently limit the potential for transformative—rather than reformative—change. Nevertheless, I take as a starting point that educational research should not only explain phenomena but also inform educational practices and organizations, and that to do so, at least some of what we write and teach should put us in honest, respectful conversations with those whose own professional practice is implicated in our scholarship. Educational research should be theoretically and methodologically robust, yet ought to be intellectually distinctive from basic scholarship for its potential for applications that bring about improvements in the real world. Whether it is to improve how practitioners are prepared or to provide fodder for reflection and professional development, we need to speak truth to the powers that be within educational institutions.

These views are consistent with those of Carter and Reardon (2014), who argued that to improve education, we need more research framing inequality as a cultural phenomenon emerging from elites' roles crafting education policy and enacting practice that maintains inequality. Such research will be unlikely to shake loose institutionalized inequalities, however, unless the education research community also has theoretically informed approaches for engaging with education practitioners and other audiences whose behavior may be connected to the inequities we uncover. I consider this a challenge of praxis, of translating research to practice in ways that foster change in the relationships and structures that shape educational and, by extension, other opportunities. My goal with this chapter is to advance educational scholars' capacity for such research.

I build the case that relational sociology can move qualitative researchers of education toward praxis by reframing a tension between constructivist and critical paradigms that can accompany qualitative inquiry into "top-down inequalities." Studies of institutionalized inequality often require scholars to identify problematic behaviors, unexamined attitudes, or inherited assumptions among powerful actors (e.g., teachers, faculty, educational administrators). However, should they learn new behaviors, attitudes, and assumptions, the same people may become key players in reducing inequities and improving education. The possibility that practitioners will engage seriously with our findings and reevaluate their assumptions and practices may hinge on our theoretical choices as scholars. I propose that theoretical perspectives from relational sociology are fruitful for this type of research due to their more dynamic conceptualizations of power. Broadly, relational sociology depicts power in and responsive to connections, transactions, and relationships, rather than painting power as a substance or property inherent in individual people and their behaviors. This paradigm, then, is not shy to address power, and its reformulation of the construct (Emirbayer 1997) provides a framework for constructive confrontation (Burgess & Burgess 1996) that is amenable to practitioners' reflection and behavioral change.

The chapter's title is adapted from the Quaker call to "speak truth to power." Educational stratification scholars need theoretical paradigms that speak truth to power, yet are sensitive to the implications of which truths they speak, for as bell hooks observed, "If I do not speak in a language that can be understood, there is little possibility of dialogue." I take the epistemological stance that the theoretical and methodological orientations we choose will shape which truths we see in the social world, and thus which truths we communicate. I do not address communication of our research with nonprofessional communities who might also contribute to institutional change in education. Nor do I try to tackle all possible relational views or cast them simultaneously as equally relevant, given the considerable heterogeneity among them. For example, prominent scholars identified in Emirbayer's (1997) review as holding relational views of power vary in casting them as macro-level, structural relationships (e.g., Bourdieu analyzes competitive relationships within both defined "fields of power" and unbounded institutional fields like schooling, generally) or micro-level understandings and interactions (e.g., Foucault explores "relations of power" through the cognitive disequilibria they can induce). I intend to highlight how relational sociology's reformulation of power provides a lens for (1) understanding thorny problems of elite educators' practice and (2) constructively confronting and engaging with them to support their learning and thus destabilize institutionalized inequalities.

As I describe in the next section, the first task is naming the power dynamics behind oppression and top-down inequalities, which sociological conflict theories have long explored. I then describe constructivist and critical paradigms for qualitative research and the dilemma for praxis they may present in studies of educational inequalities. I describe the potential of relational sociological perspectives—especially about power—to resolve this tension for qualitative researchers. Finally, I illustrate the dilemma and its resolution by looking at the same set of ethnographic field notes from constructivist, critical, and relational standpoints. I close by reflecting on the ethical implications for researchers and practical implications for our engagement with educators as learners.

Foundations in Sociological Conflict Theory

What I am proposing here is a way for educational researchers to think about pragmatic resistance—how we might use our research to constructively confront educational practices that reproduce inequalities and other power asymmetries. To that end, the foundations of my argument lie in sociological conflict theories and its modern applications in scholarship on conflict management, which highlight conflict and confrontation as tools for balancing power asymmetries of many sorts. These principles also provide a framework for how to conceptualize interactions with practitioners in educational institutions, which I revisit later in the chapter.

Marx argued that competition for limited resources puts society in a state of perpetual conflict. Typically, those with power and other resources do whatever it takes to maintain them, including acting in their own self-interest. As collective consciousness of their oppression comes to light, Marx argued, revolution by the proletariat—not gradual change—can redress power and resource asymmetries, at least temporarily. However, history shows such instances are rare. When social changes occur, even through progressive social movements, incremental change is observed at least as often as abrupt, revolutionary change because processes for allocating power often involve negotiation and compromise.

Whereas Marx focused on material resources as the basis for struggles for power, Weber's formulation extended conflict theory to acknowledge layers of conflict between those with more and less power, which interactively shape how domination is exercised and thus stratification maintained. His three-component theory of stratification documented how wealth, power, and status work together and the emotional components of conflict and resistance "that make 'legitimacy' a crucial focus for efforts at domination" (Collins & Sanderson 2015, n.p.). When we make status and legitimacy part of the conversation about power, conflict is recognized as more than a struggle for material resources. The intrapsychic stake that people have in systems of power becomes clear, and interactions (even those with some element of conflict) and emotions underlying them become tools by which solidarity across status groups can form and new forms of legitimate practice can take hold. Managing interactions with powerful groups, however, is key to the potential for constructive confrontation and conflict to step out of their own self-interest and build solidarity. I turn now to discuss how the theoretical paradigms that frame our research may contribute to such interactions with elites.

Theoretical Paradigms in Qualitative Stratification Research

Different forms of scholarly research make different knowledge contributions. A distinctive contribution to knowledge that qualitative research can make is generating hypotheses through which theory is formed and refined (Charmaz 2014; Corbin & Strauss 2015). A National Science Foundation workshop on standards for qualitative research also concludes that theory should inform qualitative research projects at all levels, including the research questions we articulate, the research designs we craft, and the analyses we conduct (Lamont & White 2009). Theoretical paradigms can affect the tone with which we write, the data and themes we emphasize, and even our dispositions toward research participants and others in similar positions. These factors figure prominently into the potential that our work can have in informing ongoing dialogue with educators on the ground. Two methodological traditions that are commonly drawn on to inform qualitative research in education today—either explicitly or implicitly—are constructivism and critical theory.

Constructivist Qualitative Research

Constructivism, a central paradigm of qualitative research, acknowledges that there are multiple truths and realities that derive claims for legitimacy from alignment with the social world as specific social actors experience it. Qualitative research under this paradigm thus recognizes the social contingency of knowledge and strives for narrative that sticks closely to the world as participants themselves tend to see it. In their book, *Negotiating the Complexities of Qualitative Research in Higher Education*, Jones, Torres, and Arminio (2013) discuss ethical dimensions of qualitative analysis and interpretation: "Analyzing and interpreting data carry with them a significant ethical responsibility to tell the story of the research and the participants who are part of a study in a way that participants themselves recognize as their story" (189). They note that foregrounding participant views is especially important in constructivist approaches, which immerse readers in the world as respondents understand and experience it. The constructivist paradigm holds that individuals' voices, along with their personal narratives and meanings, make up valuable knowledge and must not be excluded from educational researchers' narratives (Hatch 2002). This principle grounds many qualitative research methodologies (Denzin & Lincoln 2005).

However, in studies of institutionalized inequality whose participants have privileged status, a constructivist perspective may yield findings with the same blind spots toward power and privilege that elites themselves often have. Participants may express socially acceptable rationales for otherwise unacceptable behaviors or may fail to see their contributions to and complicity in institutionalized systems of inequity. As a result, grounding research understandings in their voices may mask the need for change or misrecognize avenues for achieving it.

Critical Qualitative Research

Critical qualitative methodologies often bring to the general constructivist approach a sensitivity to power, an explicit effort to interrogate dominant narratives, or commitment to centering and amplifying the voices of historically marginalized populations (e.g., Hatch 2002; Solórzano & Yosso 2002;). Though the tradition of critical research defies easy definition due to constant changes and purposeful disagreements, its roots in the years immediately following World War I are clear. Challenging Marxist orthodoxy in the face of repeated failures by strikes and protests in Europe to achieve their goals, members of the Frankfurt School held fast to their beliefs that entrenched systems of power and oppression shape lived experience. Education researchers have continued the critical tradition in various ways,[2] such as by highlighting the tensions between schools as sites of domination and reproduction, as Bowles and Gintis (1976) famously argued, but also as sites of possible transformation. Culturally relevant and liberatory pedagogy, for example, can empower students and other actors in education to critically think about and stand up to unjust political, economic, and social systems (e.g., Freire 1993, 1996; Giroux 1988).

In qualitative research about top-down and institutionalized inequalities, a critical perspective holds promise as a counterpoint or corrective to constructivism. By clarifying relatively durable dynamics of power and privilege, it explains how systemic inequities often persist even amid rhetorics of egalitarianism and diversity (Kincheloe & McLaren 2002, 88). Lewis and Diamond (2015) offer a powerful example of critical qualitative research. They highlight how wealthy white parents' unreflective tendency to push for what they think is best for their high school children contributes to a broader process of opportunity hoarding that maintains racial and curricular inequalities within the walls of a school that prides itself on diversity.

Whereas constructivism can fall short in explaining top-down inequality, uncritically adopting a critical perspective may impede productive responses to it. Freire (1996) argued, "The mistake of the Left is its dogmatic and aggressive discourse" (84), and indeed, discourse focused on systems of oppression and domination may keep practitioners working within such systems from engaging with our work. It can transform "the story of the research," as Jones et al. (2013) put it, into one in which elites are unable to see themselves or in which present power dynamics as virtually untouchable. Either of these may alienate the very actors whose behavior and ways of seeing the world need to change. Research participants and readers in similar roles may reject findings out of hand rather than reflect on their relevance for improving their work.

Bringing Relationships Back In: The Potential of Relational Sociology

My experience translating research to practice on matters related to graduate admissions with professors from across the disciplines tells me that (1) as education researchers, we can and should resist respectability politics or pandering to powerful people so our work is more palatable, and (2) reaching professionals with qualitative research about the work they do (especially those who may be skeptical of qualitative research or see themselves as insiders and us as outsiders) is a relational task, one that requires smart, respectful dialogue. Leading such dialogue requires thoughtful framing and language choices as well as a posture of engagement that pairs confidence in the quality and conclusions of our work with humility about the limits of its generalizability. We will never satisfy everyone by the choices we make, but we can be strategic about the kind of conversation we encourage—namely, one that encourages reflection, critical consciousness, and thus willingness to rethink taken-for-granted behaviors.

For qualitative scholars, whether our theoretical choices implicitly rationalize the status quo, alienate key audiences, or kindle reflection will affect possibilities for dialogue about pressing problems and the potential for collective action toward solutions. Broadly, constructivism is sensitive to multiple truths, but it evades questions of power. Critical theory speaks truth to power but essentializes power. To complement the strengths of these approaches and correct for their weaknesses, we need an orientation to research that depicts social reality as dynamic and nondeterministic, and as constructed by people through transactions and relationships. Such an orientation should also acknowledge the undeniable role that power plays in institutionalizing inequality as the normal state of affairs, while making space for the embedded agency and collective creativity for change that can emerge when stakeholders leverage networks of relationships in solidarity.

How do relational sociologists conceive of power? According to Emirbayer (1997), it is not a "concept of substance," but a "concept of relationship" (291). Thus, power may be expressed in both the intersubjective interpretations that people constantly make and in the ensuing relationships they make (and unmake). Power is thus socially situated and contingent, because these interpretations and relationships reflect the performance of roles associated with salient identities (both those a person feels and those imposed on them). A Goffmanian relational perspective thus might compel the researcher to look for power in the typical scripts that members perform for each other (Goffman 1959).

Scholarship on top-down educational stratification processes can thus benefit from relational sociology in two ways. First, the anti-essentialist ontology of relational sociology, viewing social reality as a process of interactions within webs of social relations (see chapter 1 in this volume), can contextualize power dynamics and the behavior of elite actors. Such contextualization permits a wider framing and thus a more comprehensive picture of power and its manipulation. It also supports the development of research narratives that do not shy away from questions of power but center power in relationships and social processes. Relative to critical theory's more deterministic portrayal of power, a relational narrative about institutionalized inequality may better support reflection or changes in practice among educators.

This distinction is more than rhetorical. Relational views of reality and power embed researchers in the phenomenon at hand which, as I discuss in detail below, carries implications both for documenting findings and engaging with practitioners. A sense of connection to the systems we study and their problems of inequality can compel research designs that privilege engagement with participants and related audiences—in this case, education professionals of various sorts. Other research frameworks have posited the importance of constructing the researcher/participant in this way. For example, early feminist researchers' sensitivity to the ethical implications of research drove the development of methods like focus groups, which highlight participants' experiential knowledge and reduce the risk of exploitation in the researcher–subject relationship. Today, critical indigenous research methodology (CIRM) similarly strives to embed researcher/subject reciprocity as one of its four key values (Brayboy, Gough, Leonard, Roehl, & Solyom 2012). CIRM thus employs mechanisms such as member checking, which facilitate coconstruction of the findings and mutual benefit.

To summarize, relational sociology offers an interpretive framework attuned to power and privilege, fostering the connection and dialogue that social change requires. It creates common ground, shifts the researcher's positioning relative to respondents and the data, and acknowledges the complex social relations with which systems of power operate.

An Illustration from Elite Decision Making

To illustrate the implications for facing inequality and encouraging ongoing dialogue that these different theoretical perspectives may have, I interpret from three angles—constructivist, critical, and relational—an episode from a recent comparative ethnographic study of doctoral admissions decision making. Then I analyze how implications for practice vary with each perspective. First, I selected an evocative episode from one of the ten case studies—each of which had been member checked with the admissions committee or department chair. This step was effectively a sampling decision because it elicited the "data" I interpret. My selection criteria were twofold. One, the episode and case study needed to emerge from a combination of observational and interview data, and two, the episode represented the general findings from the broader study: through their deliberations, faculty construct a facially neutral ideal of "merit" that may nevertheless perpetuate unequal enrollment. My analytic goal was to understand why two students who would contribute to the department's diversity goals were nonetheless denied admission.

It bears noting that as a woman and long-standing social justice advocate, I tend toward critical interpretations of social life and research data. However, as a White-identified professor affiliated with a research university, I also bring a standpoint to research that could incline me to the same myopia about privilege that I am concerned about in my research participants—the majority of whom are White men in research universities. As a check on this possibility, I have solicited input on this work at each step of the research process from a racially/ethnically diverse group of scholars.

Talking Risk in the Humanities

In the following episode, faculty in a top-ranked humanities department debate whether to admit two applicants who had been recruited through a department-level diversity initiative. I call the students Alicia and Joanne. Both students were first-generation, low-income women attending a nearby college. Both had some experience with research from courses, but unlike some of this PhD program's applicants, they did not yet have a record of publication. One member of the committee mentioned Joanne's ethnicity (Native American), but no one spoke of Alicia's. Faculty dubbed both of them "diversity candidates," and both were finishing degrees at a nearby urban college with which this highly selective department is striving to develop a stronger relationship.

More than many other applicants under consideration by the department that year, the decisions about Alicia's and Joanne's admissions generated extended discussion—even disagreement and debate—among the faculty. Their admissions committee chair, whom I call Peter, explained to me:

> We got from the graduate school a diversity grant. We decided to interpret diversity broadly, not just race and gender and all those things. We have very few students from local colleges, so we contacted a college right in the heart of the city, and we told them that if they have good undergraduates to apply

> here because there's this image that we are snobby so there is no point to apply here. So we had several applications from this college and two made the short list.

Indeed, the previous year they did admit one student from the college. This time, although a majority of the committee had voted in their initial meeting for Alicia and Joanne to be put on the short list, a majority raised serious concerns when deciding whether they should be invited for the campus visit weekend that they used to screen students before making final admissions decisions. Some committee members thought that one student's research interests were not clearly enough articulated. Some felt the other student constituted too much of a risk, academically.

After reviewing Joanne's basic credentials, the department chair commented, "If we're serious about diversity, these are the kind of students we need to take seriously." A professor who hadn't yet spoken in the meeting interrupted, "Can I please speak up? We want diversity, but we want excellence in diversity. And when I read that statement, it was all over the place." Another person affirmed, "We need evidence of research skill, which we had with both of the last two applicants we discussed." A third added, "I tried to talk with her when she visited campus and couldn't get a line." After a pause, Nancy, a senior member of the committee, proposed a relationship between diversity and perceived risk: "In most cases, diversity will involve some degree of risk on our part. We have to not be so risk averse that we miss opportunities." There was a pause in the conversation. "That's true," added Denise, one of the people who had expressed concern just moments earlier. "And students from her ethnicity are very unlikely to apply to graduate school." Unable to come to consensus, they tabled the case for a while.

Turning next to discuss Alicia, Peter read an extended portion of a letter of recommendation, which closed with the line: "I hope you get to meet her." The committee member followed his reading with, "And we will. She's coming to campus this Friday for a visit." As with Joanne, it became clear as they dug into Alicia's application that no one was firmly convinced about whether to move her forward in the process. Peter sounded unsure about her, but Denise, the department chair, highlighted the extreme personal struggles the student had faced, concluding, "She might be a bet, but it could be a good bet," and reiterated the point she made earlier, "If we are going to increase diversity, these are the students we need to take seriously." Tentatively, an Asian member of the committee who had not previously spoken in the meeting asked, "What's the diversity?" Denise and Nancy, who by then were advocating for her, responded with "family financial hardship." The committee agreed at that point to leave her on the list, and discussion about her and about building diversity continued. Nancy said, "It will be good for the whole faculty to take a look at her file. It seems pretty clear that she's a risk, but if we're going to increase diversity, we have to take risks." Concurring, Denise added, "And she seems like a good bet. Increasing diversity will also require these pipelines."

At the full faculty meeting that followed these deliberations, the committee members' colleagues voted to invite Alicia and Joanne for the official visit that would precede their final decisions. However, when the final selection occurred, the committee rejected them both. They needed to eliminate four applicants, and as Peter described it to me in a follow-up interview, "in the first five minutes, with very little discussion" they decided Alicia and Joanne should be two of them. He offered some additional detail to me, explaining:

> PETER: There was universal agreement about two of them. There were just two students that no one thought were up to the bar. So that got us down to ten. We liked them both, [but] we thought they didn't have the intellectual capacity to excel in graduate school.
>
> JULIE: And what was it during the campus visit that gave you the sense of that?
>
> PETER: . . . In the end they just didn't have the right preparation. They were just, there were others from universities with great, active linguistics departments where they probably had taken two years' worth of graduate courses already, things like that. The local students just didn't have that preparation. So they might have been perfectly capable, but in comparison. . . . We felt horrible. We really wanted them, but it just wasn't going to happen. . . . I'm still wondering what necessarily the right thing to do is. Both of them may have had the intellectual ability, but they didn't have as much background as the other students. So maybe if there were a way to guarantee them a sixth year of funding so that they can take an extra year to catch up, but that's not something we have.

My follow-up interview with another committee member supported this recollection. This White man said:

> There were applicants that we were hoping to be able to take a chance on that we invited to campus. Sadly, once they got here we decided it would not be a good gamble. Um, and in fact I mean, we really were *disappointed* because we did personally *like* the people involved and a lot about them, but again you have to think about what you're doing to their lives as well. [*Pause*] But so some of the sort of last stage of discussion was which of the people that sort of might fit in that category are likely to be a good enough risk?

Before he changed the topic, we went on to talk more about the idea of risk, the assumptions that constitute perceived risk, and the difficulties of gauging it. Like Peter, his body language and stilted speech clearly communicated his discomfort with the outcomes for Joanne and Alicia—and his discomfort discussing it with me.

Interpretations and Their Implications

Interpreting this episode from the three theoretical perspectives yields different answers to the question of why the committee rejected Alicia and Joanne. A constructivist perspective construes the decision as a discursive process of meaning making. A critical perspective might cast the outcome as a result of structural classism, sexism, or racism that reproduces elite interests and opportunities. A relational perspective, finally, would understand the decision as a dynamic struggle among the interconnected members of the admissions committee. Here, I outline these interpretations in greater detail and note the different implications for decision making and decision makers that accompany each.

Constructivist. Three discursive themes emerge from a constructivist perspective: participants' repeated construction of these prospective students in relation to risk and diversity, the central role they give to "intellectual ability" among their selection preferences, and their framing of academic excellence and diversity as competing interests. I note how members of this committee grapple with the desire to maximize both excellence and diversity, but by defining the former only in relation to their assumptions about intellectual ability, they construct excellence and diversity as a trade-off. "We want diversity, but we want excellence in diversity," one committee member said, with others offering supportive remarks. On the other hand, participants see diversity and risk as intertwined, so that comments like, "In most cases, diversity will involve some degree of risk on our part" could be met with nodding from around the table. From this perspective, the diversity they seek is difficult to achieve because actors perceive it to be more of a risk than a benefit to the university's core interest in academic excellence.

Implications of this perspective for decision making are largely discursive and consistent with the "small wins" perspective articulated by Karl Weick (1984). He argues we can do something about large, complex, seemingly intractable social problems by redefining the meanings that key actors attribute to the ideas that drive construction of problems and avenues for their solution. In this case, redefining the meanings and relationships of excellence, ability, diversity, and risk might change the terms of the conversation about so-called borderline applicants in ways that produce different actions on such individuals—toward outcomes that chip away at inequality instead of reinforce it. The education scholar engaging with practitioners could press them to improve their practice by urging them to examine the evidentiary basis for their assumptions, such as about the relationship of indicators of ability to actual performance in graduate school.

Critical. Centering my attention on structural, enduring power relationships based on race, class, or gender puts the micro-level conversations that led to Alicia's and Joanne's rejection decisions in a different light, as well as their implications. The outcome can be understood, at its core, to represent the reproduction of elite interests and opportunities. Interpretation might yield the same general observations as a constructivist lens when it comes to discourses of diversity, excellence, and risk, for example, but the critical lens would also enable me to locate those discourses within metanarratives and ideologies of merit that are not neutral from the perspective of structural inequities. Such narratives have been constructed to serve the interests of the populations who more often enroll in postsecondary institutions like the research university I was studying. Furthermore, they often impede opportunities for students who enroll in less-resourced colleges like the one the prospective students in question were attending. The critical perspective thus highlights that inequities in representation are reproduced through shared blind spots in the facially neutral dynamics of decision making, especially the perceived legitimacy of narratives to which people at the table tend to tacitly defer.

Second, a critical paradigm may also notice and consider how structural inequalities are reflected in the group's composition. Specifically, acknowledging that this is a setting in which participants are allocating scarce opportunities attunes me to who has voice and authority to shape the conversations that determine admission fates. Rereading the case study for who is present and absent in these deliberations, I notice that the committee consists mostly of men and that conversation around the table is dominated by men. I might infer (albeit without explicit evidence) that this may explain why few comments go unchallenged. A critical race perspective might draw my attention to the fact that there was just one person of color in the room—a man from China with a heavy accent—and that in a long meeting he spoke only once, in the form of a question. The absence of US-born women of color on the committee—and in the department—positions Alicia and Joanne as members of an out-group.

Implications for decision making that follow from the critical perspective center on the need to shift admissions decision-making power away from historically overrepresented groups and assert the legitimacy of counternarratives about merit and excellence. Wealthy white men—by virtue of their disproportionate presence in the academy—have had power historically to shape the terms of access to higher education and, today, people who share those social identities (individually or in combination) are disproportionately represented on the committee. Drawing from Kanter's (1977) work on critical mass, an education scholar working with this committee could press the chair to reassess the processes by which they select who serves on the admissions committee so that the populations they want to enroll are well represented in the group. However, given empirical literature that professionals from historically marginalized groups do not always advocate for others who share their identity—and in some cases may even be harsher judges—a different view of how power is operating in the group may be needed.

Relational. Considering the decision making about admitting Alicia and Joanne from a relational perspective highlights the collective nature of evaluation and selection, as well as the struggle among group members that unfolds through their interactions and negotiations. As discussed earlier, a distinctive conceptualization of power drives the relational interpretation. According to this view, power is not a static property established in enduring social hierarchies and held to varying degrees based on one's social identities, but is threaded through the dyadic and group interactions by which admissions becomes an institutionalized compromise across many interests. Power is expressed, spent, produced, and amplified moment to moment in acts of persuasion and in the exchanges of social capital that advocacy for or against an applicant entails. It is thus related to constructivism's focus on discourse and to critical theory's focus on power, but it is distinctive from each.

Returning to a Goffmanian relational perspective, I saw several scripts play out repeatedly in this committee's interactions. (1) Jump in and express support immediately after a view you like is expressed, to build momentum or affirm your relationship with the person who expressed it. (2) If the goal is to introduce doubt in colleagues' minds about an applicant, appeal to perceived risk that the applicant poses to shared values (e.g., confidence about degree completing, sophistication, intelligence). (3) lay nicely, but edge out a colleague, acknowledge a point of agreement before introducing a contrary view. (4) To distract from an emerging narrative that counters one's own opinion about a student's admissibility, use humor or otherwise redirect the committee member's attention. In this playbook, such scripts link power and discourse, recognizing that actors perform the scripts they hold to be in accordance with their roles, on one hand, and their desired aims in the moment, on the other.

In this episode, I see power through comments that affirm alliances within the committee, through the application of pressure to clarify the grounds for claims made, and through challenges to conventional wisdom. Although debates about the applicants in relation to excellence and diversity can still be linked to broader narratives about ability and risk, a relational view highlights that these narratives are being tweaked and rewritten in vivo, as group members define and redefine whom the department sees itself to be presently and in relation to what it wants to be with respect to diversity. Increasing diversity requires different engagement with students and institutional pipelines they might have otherwise overlooked: "If we are going to increase diversity, these are the students we need to take seriously," and "Increasing diversity will also require these pipelines." In contrast to a view that emphasizes critical mass, presence for decision making matters not only because it is expected that people will have particular preferences based on their identities, but also because they have the opportunity to reinforce, challenge, or rewrite prevailing narratives through their discussions. In these respects, a relational perspective on the outcome of their deliberations emphasizes the discussion's emergent, transactional qualities, and the embedded agency of group members. In the case at hand, deciding not to admit Alicia and Joanne on the basis of questions about their "intellectual ability" can be understood to say as much about the faculty members as it does about the prospective students.

Ethical Implications for Researchers of a Relational Perspective

The relational view just described carries ethical implications for me as an education researcher and practical implications for readers of the work, which this section and the next delineate in turn. Simply noting that "the researcher sees power" highlights a particular ontological stance and implies scholarly responsibility. The quality of my own vision for these complex social dynamics will be contingent on my identities to some unknown degree, as well as on my effort to refine a theoretical perspective, or lens, through which power is a product of more than my idiosyncratic perspective. My ability to document the most salient intragroup power dynamics depends on how well I have come to understand what is typical for interactions and relationships in this group. Extended periods of observation help me "see power."

Moreover, by shifting my view of power from a form of property to a force that permeates interactions, I feel an ethical obligation to hold leadership accountable for those interactions. I am personally predisposed to valuing interactions that support more equitable outcomes, and this starts with encouraging more open-minded attitudes about who can succeed in graduate school. This disposition, with a relational perspective, drives me to highlight how each person's actions and attitudes—as well as their interactions and relationships—affect which narratives are constructed and which ones drive decisions. However, the committee chair guides collective decision making in a special way. His power inheres in shaping the committee's exchange, and thus the shared understandings that emerges about each student and about merit generally. Given the typical style of interactions in this group, the chair appeared to be the only one with full agency to interrupt and redirect the flow of collective understanding toward different outcomes—yet he almost never did so.

Finally and fundamentally, a relational perspective helps me appreciate my relationships with the participants in this study. That appreciation shifts my mindset, and I see the respondents and data differently. A recognition of our common role as faculty members in research universities enables me to position this group not only as my subjects but on some level as professional colleagues—as "we," not "they." This shift in mindset nudges me to consider how my assumptions about excellence, diversity, or risk may inform my interpretations of their discussions and how I weave together the details to write up the episode. Seeing myself in relationship with participants also compels me to situate the committee's discussion of these students and of diversity in light of the current legal and political contexts for admissions and affirmative action. The reminder that I am there as a participant/observer inspires gratitude that I was permitted to observe the conversation at all and sparks desire to understand as deeply as possible to encourage dialogue about how we could more effectively link recruitment and admissions efforts. In short, whereas a straightforward critical perspective gave me eyes for the committee's shortcomings, adding a relational perspective enabled me to see the committee's potential and capacity with one another and the imperative of improving a system of which I am, on some level, also a part.

Practical Implications for Decision Making of a Relational Perspective

The utility for faculty of reading an episode like this rests on its potential to stimulate reflection that shapes how professors act in similar situations. I highlight three ways I believe that actors present in the conversation could have acted and interacted differently. First, as explained already, I would note that the committee chair, Peter—whose desire to grow as a higher education leader was plain to me in our interviews—could certainly have taken a more active role shaping (a) the exchange of ideas and viewpoints, (b) the negotiations about what can be inferred from a student's file or from meeting them briefly, and (c) the compromises across multiple priorities that emerged from the committee's discussions.

I would also propose that committee chairs and academic leaders generally attune themselves to the cumulative import of micro-level interactions. Through them, discussions in routine meetings can reproduce, challenge, and re-create wider narratives about merit and student potential.

Finally, this episode can help professors see how the interactions that led to Alicia and Joanne's rejection are not independent from the institutional relationships that reproduce broader organizational hierarchies in higher education. I would encourage readers in elite universities to discuss how their usual admissions priorities enable or constrain them from establishing the sort of mutually respectful relationships they say they want to develop. Strengthening those relationships may lead members of this department to take a different view of the "intellectual ability" of students.

Conclusion

In the years that qualitative methodologies have come to the mainstream of education research, feminist and Indigenous researchers "have won recognition that the same phenomenon viewed from different standpoints can produce different 'truths'—all of them with legitimate claims to validity" (Castellano, 2008, 427). Just as there is not a single "best" interpretation of the episode I described, there is not a single best paradigm for educational research. I hope to have demonstrated that although typical education research training rightfully encourages us to design studies with an eye to the research question at hand, in our design choices we should also attend to prospects for ongoing dialogue with practitioners. Relational sociology's ontology yields a view of power, and thus research findings, that are conducive to faculty reflection, dialogue, and intervention. Education researchers can take away three key points from this chapter.

The theoretical and methodological choices we make, while centered on answering research questions, also carry consequences for the kinds of truths we are likely to uncover. Some truths lead to more productive conversations, and if we want to challenge educational inequality as it manifests in practice, we need a framework that elevates the importance of both interactions and power.

Relational sociology offers a constructive approach to confronting power. For social phenomena like admissions, in which negotiations among people near the top of status hierarchies determine access and opportunity, we need to change the nature of the negotiations that occur and the narratives that emerge from it. These are questions of power that demand theoretical perspectives that are sensitive to it. Relational sociology defines power not as a static property of individuals and organizations reflected in endemic status hierarches but as a dynamic force that permeates group interactions and relationships. It shares with critical perspectives attention to power, and shares with constructivism attention to discourse; thus, it captures social reality in ways that constructivism and critical perspectives may miss. What is more, the recognition that power is constantly being exchanged, created, and spent in relationships and interactions offers a productive stance for engaging with practitioners by keeping the focus on behavior and transactions rather than on implicit or explicit claims about intrinsic qualities of people (which may put people on the defensive) or of groups (that so often deny their heterogeneity). Emirbayer (1997) noted that relational perspectives enable productive attention to "intrapsychic processes" that "see transactions with others, and not pregiven drives" (297) as the basis for power. Ideally, at least, such a view opens those engaged in the conversation to begin appreciating their connections with one another—that is, to begin appreciating the potential for collective interests and solidarity. Only when this occurs, can we begin pursuing transactions that take the form Emirbayer (1997) imagines, of "free and open communication of actors in a universal community, a relational matrix within which both cooperation and conflict are rationally regulated" (310). For the potential that this view of power holds to establish the grounds for collective action, we need to put it to work more often in our work on inequality.

Finally, our capacity to facilitate research-informed discussions on matters of educational practice, is a key expression of our own power as scholars. We who study inequalities in education can maximize the value of our work through engagement with people who are implicated in the injustices our research uncovers. Such engagement helps fulfill our obligation as scholars to support the transformation (not just description) of institutionalized inequities and systems of power. As an applied field of study, education scholars have an ethical obligation to unearth and reflect back to practitioners aspects of their work that are embedded as the normal state of affairs but that institutionalize inequities. Relational perspectives enable us to portray evidence in ways that acknowledge complexity, to respect respondents' understanding of their social worlds, and to engage them as coconstructors in problem solving. Such translational work is part of what constitutes excellent education research today. It forces us to communicate more clearly and increases the relevance of our work for policy and practice.

Notes

1. "Certain members of the oppressor class join the oppressed in their struggle for liberation. . . . Theirs is a fundamental role, and has been so throughout the history of this struggle. It happens, however, that as they cease to be exploiters or indifferent spectators or simply the heirs of exploitation and move to the side

of the exploited, they must always bring with them the marks of their origin: their prejudices and their deformations, which include a lack of confidence in the people's ability to think, to want, and to know. Accordingly these adherents to the people's cause constantly run the risk of falling into a type of generosity as malefic as that of the oppressors. . . . [They] truly desire to transform the unjust order; but because of their background they believe that they must be the executors of the transformation. They talk about the people but they do not trust them; and trusting the people is the indispensable precondition for revolutionary change" (Freire 1993, 60).

2. Hammersley (2005) identified four distinct stances in the critical qualitative research community: (1) gathering knowledge from disciplinary standpoints, (2) change-minded policy research, (3) research that destabilizes current discourse, and (4) using qualitative methods to speak to current issues.

References

Bowles, S., & Gintis, H. (1976). *Schooling in capitalist America*. New York, NY: Basic Books.

Brayboy, B. M. J., Gough, H. R., Leonard, B., Roehl, I. I., Roy, F., & Solyom, J. A. (2012). Reclaiming scholarship: Critical indigenous research methodologies. In *Qualitative research: An introduction to methods and designs*, edited by S. D. Lapan, M. T. Quartaroli, and F. J. Reimer, 423–50. San Francisco, CA: Jossey-Bass.

Burgess, H., & Burgess, G. (1996). Constructive confrontation: A transformative approach to intractable conflicts. *Mediation Quarterly*, *13*(4), 305–22.

Carter, P., & Reardon, S. (2014). *Inequality matters.* William T. Grant Foundation Inequality Paper. Available at http://wtgrantfoundation.org/inequality-matters-framing-a-strategic-inequality-research-agenda.

Castellano, M. B. (2008). Indigenous research. In *The SAGE Encyclopedia of Qualitative Research Methods*, edited by L. M. Given, 424–29. Thousand Oaks, CA: Sage.

Charmaz, K. (2014). *Constructing grounded theory*. Thousand Oaks, CA: Sage.

Collins, R., & Sanderson, S. K. (2015). *Conflict sociology: A sociological classic updated*. New York, NY: Routledge.

Corbin, J., & Strauss, A. (2015). *Basics of qualitative research: Techniques and procedures for developing grounded theory*. Thousand Oaks, CA: Sage Publications

Denzin, N. & Lincoln, Y. (2005). *The SAGE handbook of qualitative research.* Thousand Oaks, CA: Sage.

Emirbayer, M. (1997). Manifesto for a relational sociology. *American Journal of Sociology*, *103*(2), 281–317.

Freire, P. (1993). *Pedagogy of the oppressed*. 1970. New York, NY: Continuum.

Freire, P. (1996). *Letters to Cristina: Reflections on my life and work.* New York, NY: Routledge.

Giroux, H. A. (1988). *Teachers as intellectuals: Toward a critical pedagogy of learning.* Westport, CT: Greenwood Publishing.

Goffman, E. (1959). *The presentation of self in everyday life.* New York, NY: Anchor Books.

Hammersley, M. (2008). *Questioning qualitative inquiry: Critical essays.* Sage.

Hatch, J. A. (2002). *Doing qualitative research in education settings.* Albany, NY: State University of New York Press.

hooks, bell. (1995). *Killing rage: Ending racism.* New York, NY: Holt.

Jones, S. R., Torres, V., & Arminio, J. (2013). *Negotiating the complexities of qualitative research in higher education: Fundamental elements and issues.* New York, NY: Routledge.

Kanter, R. M. (1977). Some effects of proportions on group life. In *The gender gap in psychotherapy*, 53–78. Boston, MA: Springer,

Karabel, J. (2005). *The chosen: The hidden history of admission and exclusion at Harvard, Yale, and Princeton.* Boston, MA: Houghton Mifflin Harcourt.

Kincheloe, J. L., & McLaren, P. (2002). Rethinking critical theory and qualitative research. In *Ethnography and schools: Qualitative approaches to the study of education*, edited by Yali Zou and Enrique (Henry) T. Trueba, 87–138. Lanham, MD: Rowman and Littlefield.

Lamont, M., & White, P. (2008). *Workshop on interdisciplinary standards for systematic qualitative research.* Washington, DC: National Science Foundation.

Lareau, A. (2011). *Unequal childhoods: Class, race, and family life.* Berkeley, CA: University of California Press.

Lewis, A. E., & Diamond, J. B. (2015). *Despite the best intentions: How racial inequality thrives in good schools.* New York, NY: Oxford University Press.

Lucas, S. R. (2001). Effectively maintained inequality: Education transitions, track mobility, and social background effects. *American Journal of Sociology, 106*(6), 1642–90.

Milkman, K. L., Akinola, M., & Chugh, D. (2015). What happens before? A field experiment exploring how pay and representation differentially shape bias on the pathway into organizations. *Journal of Applied Psychology, 100*(6), 1678.

Posselt, J. R. (2016). *Inside graduate admissions: Merit, diversity, and faculty gatekeeping.* Cambridge, MA: Harvard University Press.

Solórzano, D. G., & Yosso, T. J. (2002). Critical race methodology: Counter-storytelling as an analytical framework for education research. *Qualitative Inquiry, 8*(1), 23–44.

Stevens, M. L. (2007). *Creating a class: College admissions and the education of elites.* Cambridge, MA: Harvard University Press.

Weick, K. E. (1984). Small wins: Redefining the scale of social problems. *American Psychologist, 39*(1), 40.

Chapter 4

Relational Sociology and Race Relations

Pushing the Conversation in Higher Education

ANTAR A. TICHAVAKUNDA

> What is needed is the further development of a dynamic sociological theory of race relations, which will discard all the rationalizations of race prejudice and provide orientation for the study of the constantly changing patterns of race relations in American life.
>
> —E. Franklin Frazier, *Sociological Theory and Race Relations*

White nationalists march through a college campus proclaiming, "White lives matter" (Harper & Davis 2017). Statues of Confederate soldiers and leaders stand (Stancill 2017); others are removed (Neuman, 2017). Students protest across the country against racist structures and inequitable experiences at historically White campuses (Racial tension 2015). And so it goes. The goal of this chapter is not to articulate why we study race relations on college campuses—the need is apparent and is continually conveyed in research (e.g., Harper 2012; Patton 2016; Solórzano, Ceja, & Yosso 2000; Turner 1994). The goal of this work is to employ relational sociology in two ways: (1) to question how we study race relations on college campuses and (2) to provide examples of how relational sociology can identify and analyze precise mechanisms shaping campus racial climate.

One cannot study race relations in higher education without at least partly addressing the concept of campus racial climate (see Harper & Hurtado 2007). This chapter demonstrates how relational sociology extends, challenges, and provides further nuance to campus racial climate research. Through a relational lens, I argue, we can better understand the problem of race relations on college campuses. In constructing my argument, I examine how campus racial climate is often conceptualized in substantialist terms. Next, I describe relational sociology, highlighting how campus racial climate might be recast in relational terms. Drawing from relational thinkers, especially E. Franklin Frazier and Mustafa Emirbayer, I provide a relational recasting of two popular objects of analysis in campus climate research. While highlighting campus climate research that might be considered relational, I show how a relational orientation encourages scholars to move from (1) diverse identities to diverse processes and (2) racial slights to racialized transactions.

Substances and Relations: Introducing Relational Sociology

Relational sociology has garnered more attention in recent years as a novel approach for studying diversity and race relations (e.g., Clarke & antonio 2012; Emirbayer & Desmond 2015). Despite its growing popularity, relational sociology has been critiqued for vague, sometimes competing understandings of how to use it (see Dépelteau 2015). In accordance with the other chapters in this volume, I further define relational sociology by putting it to use—recasting campus racial climate in relational terms. Although still evolving, the school of relational sociology shares certain core epistemological assumptions that guide relational inquiry. Here I clarify the language of relational sociology, providing a short background of its theoretical underpinnings as well as defining "relational thinking" and "substantialist thinking," two phrases used throughout this chapter.

Emirbayer identified two divergent approaches to sociology—the substantialist and relational approaches. Substantialist thinking, he argued, implicitly holds that social worlds are composed of substances or "static 'things,'" whereas relational thinking recognizes the social as consisting of processes and "dynamic, unfolding relations" (Emirbayer 1997, 281). Relational sociology is guided by the idea that social reality is constructed through dynamic relationships and processes. Rather than putting undue emphasis on the individual, rational action, or deterministic super structures, relational sociologists identify different objects of analysis—relationships (see Desmond 2014). A substantialist perspective, for example, views power as a possession or entity; a relational perspective views power as a dynamic relationship between various actors. Substantialist thinking is ultimately ill-equipped to analyze social realities. Desmond (2014), for example, argued that substantialism endorses "a vision of the world as a vast collection of isolated entities stacked side-by-side like so many jarred specimens on laboratory shelves" (552).

Emirbayer (1997) argued that dynamic relationships between processes and actors are the ideal objects of sociological research. Drawing from the thought of Émile Durkheim (Emirbayer 1996), Emirbayer suggested that sociologists adopt relational thinking by focusing on relations transcending individual entities or actors, as opposed to the substantialist thinking of focusing on the disparate entities themselves. Pragmatist philosophy also shaped Emirbayer's manifesto (e.g., Dewey 2008), namely, the understanding that human experience and agency occurs within a specific, temporal moment and unique context. From the relational sociologist's perspective, conceiving of agents outside of their transactional context yields little sociological usefulness (Emirbayer 1997, 287). In this manner, discrete variables, or substances, are no longer the object of research. Relational sociology also assumes that the agentic, cultural, and societal dimensions of action can work together in different ways to reinforce or alter the structured relationships between people or groups in society. A relational approach is useful in studying how discrete processes or mechanisms emerging from relations structure inequity. I highlight the relational nature of race before defining campus racial climate, showing how relational sociology can benefit campus racial climate research. The concepts outlined are also articulated in greater detail in later sections using campus racial climate research as a working example.

The Relational Nature of Race

A substantialist conception renders race static and unmoving, which is historically inaccurate and leaves us incapable of studying race relations as they evolve over time. Consider, for example, how Irish Americans became White (Ignatiev 2012). Ignatiev demonstrates how Catholic Irish escaped a racialized, caste-like oppression in Ireland and became part of the White, dominant race in North America. Irish Americans, Ignatiev argues, achieved Whiteness, not simply from their skin tone but from their antagonism and violence toward Blacks. Categorically, race is relational and in flux.

Race is not a static "thing." Race is relational, usefully analyzed as a processual, dynamic relation. Theoretically, race is understood as a relationship. For example, race—or Blackness in particular—as we know it, came to be at the onset of the transatlantic slave trade. Europeans traveling to West Africa became "White" and Africans of different ethnicities were made "Black" or "Negro" upon arriving in the Americas (see Rediker 2007). Whether through White supremacy and the domination of non-Whites (Solórzano et al. 2000), racial triangulation (Kim 1999), anti-Black antagonism (Ray, Randolph, Underhill, & Luke 2017), or racial projects (Omi & Winant 2014), race is theorized with relationships in mind. Relational sociology can be used as a supplement to such theories. White supremacy, for example, is sometimes constructed as a substance. Relational sociology provides another level of nuance, identifying and centering on the patterned relationships that structure White supremacy and other relationships inherent in theories of race.

Relational sociology is also useful to study relations across categorical identities within a racial group. The Black community, for example, is not a substance but a dynamic relation with fractures, boundaries, and bonds. A relational approach takes stock of the social positioning of people within groups—for example, the social position of a Black man is different from that of a Black woman. With relational sociology, a scholar is attuned to the processes that shape Black collectives or perhaps the boundary-making processes within groups. The intersectional nature of identity comes to the forefront with a relational perspective.

When understood as a substance, race becomes a variable, something a scholar might control for in a study. Understanding race as a substance has the potential to divorce it from its historical context, thereby neglecting the material legacies of structural oppression and domination. Relational sociology, however, centers the inherently relational nature of race. Given the potential of relational sociology in studying racial realities, I narrow my focus, examining how relational sociology might be used to study campus racial climates in particular.

Campus Racial Climate and the Potential of Relational Sociology

Racialized experiences, tensions, and relations display different qualities depending on institution type. This chapter focuses on campus climate research at historically White institutions of higher education (HWIs). While predominantly White institutions (PWIs) report at least a 50 percent White student population, HWIs might report less than a 50 percent White student population and have a history of excluding/limiting the numbers of non-White students (see Allen, Epps, & Haniff 1991). In this text, I use HWIs expansively to include PWIs given their shared tradition of alienating non-White students.

HWIs across the country have unique characteristics, yet certain trends concerning campus racial climate exist. Research shows that students of different races often experience the same campus—its institutions, policies, and cultures—differently, with similarities along racial lines (Harper & Hurtado 2007; Hurtado, Griffin, Arellano, & Cuellar 2008). In other words, from residence halls (Harwood, Huntt, Mendenhall, & Lewis 2012) to the financial aid office (Tichavakunda 2017), Black students and other marginalized populations at HWIs potentially experience campus institutions differently and in a negative, racialized manner. White students tend to perceive race relations and the campus climate to be more positive than do their Black and Latinx counterparts (Hurtado 1992).

Scholars with intentions of analyzing the racial context of higher education or the "realities of race on campus" (Harper & Hurtado 2007, 8) often invoke the campus racial climate concept. Although varying interpretations of the this concept exist (e.g., Cabrera, Nora, Terenzini, Pascarella, & Hagedorn 1999; Yosso, Smith, Ceja, & Solórzano 2009), most definitions understand campus racial climate as the racial environment or context of a campus and how campus stakeholders experience the racial context. Other times, campus racial climate is referred to by scholars but not defined.

Hurtado, Clayton-Pederson, Allen, and Millem (1998), noting the trend of scholars describing campus climate as important yet intangible, further developed the campus racial climate framework first introduced by Hurtado (1992). Their framework outlines the supposed intangible climate by identifying its multiple dimensions. In their framework, climate is constructed through external forces, such as policy and sociohistorical context, and internal forces, including structural diversity, campus histories of race relations, psychological climate, and behavioral climate (Hurtado et al. 1998). In other words, this framework understands the climate as structured by practices, policies, and actions of stakeholders on and off campus. Hurtado and colleagues (2008), in their review of climate assessments, offer a working definition of "campus racial climate": "part of the institutional context that includes community members' attitudes, perceptions, behaviors, and expectations around issues of race, ethnicity, and diversity" (205).

Campus racial climate is a foundational concept for higher education research and has led to advances in our understanding of race relations on campuses (see Harper & Hurtado 2007). The scholarly impulse, it seems, has been to understand campus racial climate as a substance rather than a relation. In the next section, I describe key concepts of relational sociology, namely, what exactly I mean when I deem an approach substantialist or relational. I argue that substantialist conceptions of campus racial climate are prevalent, limiting, and far from realizing the potential of the framework conceived by Hurtado and colleagues (1998).

Is Campus Racial Climate a Substance?

Substantialist approaches to inquiry study objects as if the social world is composed of various substances or static things. Social processes, such as campus racial climates, are given adjectives instead of careful analysis. For example, campus racial climates are often described as negative, hostile, or unwelcoming without an in-depth analysis of the relationships and resulting forces that structure the climate.

Campus climate is conceptualized as "part of an intricate web of relations, socially constructed by individuals in an environment" (Hurtado et al. 2008, 204). Most campus climate studies however, do not stray outside of examining how students perceive the campus environment (see Hurtado et al. 2008). A trend also exists of equating the whole campus climate framework with perceptions and descriptions of the racial context (see Harper & Hurtado 2007; Hurtado et al. 2008). This trend further emphasizes the point that campus racial climate, a multidimensional concept, is often studied as a substance.

As scholars continue to make a static substance out of campus climate, substantialist modes of understanding campus racial climates reign. Campus climates are "chilly" (Hall & Sandler 1982; Harper 2012), the state of race relations is poor, and so forth. Scholars have a tendency to characterize race relations or campus racial climate as smog overlaying a city—substances existing outside of people. Given the prevalence of substantialist constructions, the processual and relational nature of campus racial climates are underexamined.

Pitfalls of Substantialist Thinking

By reducing dynamic processes to static objects, analysts tend to view people as atomistic, uninvolved from larger structures (Elias 1978). In other words, a substantialist approach to studying campus racial climate implicitly views students, staff, and faculty as separate from the campus racial climate instead of inherently related to and coconstructors of the climate. Much campus racial climate research follows a similar design (see Hurtado et al. 2008). Scholars select preconstructed groups and seek to explore their perceptions of the campus racial climate. Exploring how specific students and faculty of different identities experience the campus racial climate sheds light on understudied populations. Yet adopting similar substantialist approaches yields similarly, limited substantialist findings. We learn that *x* group perceives the campus climate this way, while *y* group perceives the climate that way. The discrete processes, relationships, transactions, and temporal context that structure and restructure campus racial climates however, remain obscured in substantialist analysis. A substantialist approach disregards the interconnected reality of campus climates.

Some research invoking campus racial climate as a substance certainly has indeed yielded novel insights about how various groups differentially experience the same campus. In relying on a substantialist approach for research, however, claims are limited to an analysis that conceives of a campus racial climate as a static, macro entity separate from people. For the purpose of analysis, the substantialist approach paints the campus racial climate as its own, separate and static entity, as opposed to its true, interconnected, and dynamic social reality.

Understanding the Campus Racial Climate as a Relation

Campus climate, when understood as a substance, is something students are exposed to or experience. Like a mist shrouding the campus, students wade through the racial climate. Campus stakeholders—departments, staff, students, and others—are simply agents acted on, experiencing the climate in their own way. From a substantialist perspective, stakeholders only interact with the climate (Emirbayer 1997).

From a substantialist approach, interaction renders entities involved in an interaction static and independent of each other (Dewey & Bentley 1949). In describing substantialist research analyzing interactions, Emirbayer argued, "If anything, it is the variable attributes themselves that 'act,' that supply initiative, in interactional research" (1997, 286). Consider the trend of campus climate research. Scholars report how students of different identities experience or interact with the campus racial climate. Participants, however, are constructed as separate from the climate. Different aspects of identity, such as race or gender, then "act." In this approach, a particular characteristic (race, for example) leads to a negative perception of the climate. In other words, a student's racial identity—abstracted from the whole person—determines perception of the climate, as opposed to the dynamic forces, relationships, and specific context shaping the climate.

Recall the trends observed by Hurtado and colleagues (1998) of referring to the campus racial climate as "intangible" or likening perceptions of it as the totality of the campus racial climate framework. These trends limit the explanatory potential of campus racial climate research. Relational sociology, however, engages with both limitations. Climate becomes less intangible, and its dynamic, multidimensional qualities can be analyzed when understood relationally.

A relational approach compels the researcher to see climate as a dynamic, unfolding web of relations and transactions. A campus racial climate is thereby a relationship among faculty and students, activists and campus administrators, students of various racial groups, and other relations. As such, a relational approach mediates the false dualism between the macro-structure of climate and the student (or whatever entity, for that matter). Further engagement with the temporal nature of the campus racial climate framework is done by taking stock of the context-laden nature of action and experience (Emirbayer 1997).

Rather than ending the analysis at a description of the climate as "chilly," a relational approach seeks to identify and examine the structured relationships that alienate and exclude a particular group. Consider a case where Black students, in describing a hostile campus climate, report negative experiences with faculty. Instead of limiting data collection to students' accounts of these interactions, a relational scholar opts to make the faculty–student relationship the object of research. Using qualitative inquiry, one might interview more of the interconnected players in student–faculty interaction—students, teacher's assistants, and professors. The researcher might gain a more nuanced understanding of how the student–faculty relationship is fashioned to alienate Black students.

A relational analysis understands the climate as composed of ever-shifting relations of interconnected entities and actors. Certainly, relational sociology might be applied to campus racial climate in many ways. I provide just one example of how a relational understanding of campus racial climate is more aligned with Hurtado and colleagues' (1998) framework than other prevailing conceptions. In what follows, I show how a foundational thinker of race relations in the United States used a relational approach to provide new insights to racial life.

Relational Sociology and Race Relations

Although not necessarily identified as such, other sociologists concerned with race and race relations have used relational approaches of inquiry (e.g., Du Bois 1996; Frazier 1968; Jackson 2001). Students of the Chicago School of Sociology employed a relational view of society as early as the 1920s (see Desmond 2014; Liu & Emirbayer 2016). Chicago School sociologists adopted an ecological approach to studying social worlds, theorizing "society as interactional spaces with competing actors and fluid locations" (Liu & Emirbayer 2016, 62). Liu and Emirbayer compared ecological and Bourdieusian field analyses and concluded that although they are distinct, both approaches were relational in nature. Trained in the Chicago School, E. Franklin Frazier used an ecological (and thereby relational) approach to studying race relations and desegregation. His theoretical propositions are useful in reframing how scholars study campus racial climate.

In the mid-twentieth century, Frazier (1968) argued that race relations research had grown stagnant, lacking novel sociological insights. He pointed to two schools of sociologists: the nominalists and the realists. A nominalist viewed society as an "aggregate of individuals," believing "the key to an understanding of society is to be found in the study of the behavior of individuals as discrete units"; the realist viewed the object of research as "the social processes and the organized aspects of the collective life arising out of communication and interaction" (Frazier 1968, 43–44). The nominalist approach, Frazier explained, was an "atomistic conception which regards society as an aggregate of individuals whose behavior is to be explained in terms of the similarity of individual responses and attitudes" (1968, 4). As a result of this approach, race relations research produced little more than studies recording individuals' attitudes surrounding race as atomized units, divorced from the social reality.

Frazier critiqued studies attempting to understand racial life while simultaneously viewing people as if they lived in a vacuum. The "social reality" of race relations and the process of desegregation was left unexplored in the nominalist approach. As opposed to a nominalist view, which can be likened to the substantialist perspective, Frazier favored a different, relational approach—studying social relationships to learn more about race relations in a more dynamic manner (1968). To study the dynamic nature of race relations, Frazier believed the "characteristics of the systems of social relationships" were the proper object of analysis (1968, 9). In keeping with Desmond's guidelines of relational ethnography (2014, 556), Frazier studied how Black churches and families were shaped by the dynamics of larger social fields such as the political field or economic field. In *The Negro Family in the United States*, Frazier (1968) examined the complex relationships, history, and processes in society that shaped Black family life. In other words, Black family life was not an isolated phenomenon or substance but part of a larger ecology.

Bucking the substantialist impulse to accept the existence of groups as a given, Frazier (1968) also troubled the idea of a Black middle class, leading a sociological analysis of the practices, economic condition, social isolation, and values of the "Black bourgeoisie." In this way, he also examined the ecological process by which the Black bourgeoisie were constructed in society. His analytic focus on people as members of various social worlds, inquisitive examination of preconstructed groups (e.g., the Black middle class), and ecological approach of studying race relations are particularly informative in advancing the study of campus racial climates. In keeping with the work of Frazier and Emirbayer, I show how two different themes of campus racial climate research might be recast in more relational terms.

Rethinking Aspects of Campus Racial Climate Research

A relational recasting of campus racial climate is useful in at least two ways. First, relational sociology emphasizes relationships inherent to campus climates that are otherwise neglected. Second, a relational approach provides a theoretical orientation to move from a multidimensional framework like campus climate to a multidimensional analysis. Consider Matthew Desmond's relational approach to studying residential mobility. In broad strokes, residential mobility is multidimensional, consisting of various factors from policies to the temporal moment, to laws, to intrapersonal/community relationships or actions. Desmond (2012) argued that scholars tended to overlook mechanisms that drive residential mobility. As a result, he investigated the understudied relational process of eviction as a mechanism of residential mobility.

Desmond's approach is useful in thinking about the potential of relational sociology in campus racial climate research. To be sure, a framework of campus racial climate has been outlined and is necessarily expansive. In addressing something as large as a climate, some terms, concepts, and ideas within the framework are not fully parsed out. Similar to Desmond's observation of residential mobility research, many of the processes shaping a campus racial climate remain underexplored.

Relational sociology, I argue, has the potential to identify and analyze mechanisms, transactions, and policies that structure the campus racial climate. Research related to diversity in higher education has already begun to take a relational turn. Clarke and antonio (2012) led the charge arguing for a relational approach to studying diversity by demonstrating the benefits of network analysis. This network analytic, relational approach has already provided nuanced insights into peer effects and the processes and outcomes of friendship and relationships across racial lines in college (e.g., Bowman & Park 2014; Park 2014; Park & Kim 2013). Similarly, I argue for a relational approach in studying campus racial climate and race relations in higher education. Rather than demonstrating the benefits of a methodological approach, I conceptualize two popular objects of campus climate research in more relational terms: (1) diverse identities and (2) racial slights. In doing so, I highlight research that might be considered relational, providing novel insights to campus climate literature.

Diverse Identities to Diversity Processes

Substantive scholarly work engages with diversity and examines how diversity is "done" (e.g., Ahmed 2007; Ahmed & Swan 2006). Journals such as the *Journal of Diversity in Higher Education* are explicitly dedicated to diversity. Furthermore, research shows the benefits of positive cross-racial interactions and relationships in higher education (e.g., Gurin, Dey,

Hurtado, & Gurin 2002; Nuñez 2009). However, much of the scholarly work constructs diversity in substantialist terms. In other words, diversity is viewed as something to be achieved or found.

Substantialist constructions of diversity in this research take various forms. In some cases, diversity is understood as an identity some students have. Consider common phrases scholars sometimes use to describe certain student groups, such as "diverse populations," "students with diverse identities," or "diverse students." These constructions of diversity as a quality lend themselves to substantialist interactions in research (Dewey & Bentley 1949; Emirbayer 1997). In other words, a student's diversity, akin to a variable characteristic, promotes action or a specific practice, as opposed to a relationship in a specific context. Furthermore, identifying a student as "diverse" also leads to a vague understanding of diversity as only a "laundry list of identities" (Smith 2015, ix).

Other renderings of diversity are limited to a general demographic characteristics of populations. For example, Boelens, Voet, and De Wever, in their study on blended learning in higher education, studied in a context "situated against the background of a diverse student population" (2018, 199). In this way, diversity is understood as an essence—little more than an observation of unique demographic distributions of students' racial identities. Relatedly, Park, a noted scholar of diversity, studied to what extent students were satisfied with diversity at traditionally White institutions (2009). In this work, diversity is something to be "assembled" and "perceived." In these examples, diversity quite literally fades to the background and is constructed as a one-dimensional, static essence of a particular populations. To be sure, the substantialist construction of diversity in these studies (and many others) is not an inherent weakness, nor is my observation a challenge of the usefulness of such studies. I am only pointing out that substantialist constructions render diversity as a demographic essence. For the substantialist, diversity is seen as a positive, an achievement, a quality, or a held identity. Relational sociology, however, gives "legs" to constructions of diversity and challenges scholars to move beyond diversity as a vague descriptor.

Thinking relationally about diversity requires one to abandon readymade, static ideas of diversity (Emirbayer 1997). In a relational sense, diversity has little meaning apart from the transactions, interactions, and practices between people in a given context. Such a perspective might involve exploring the relationships between races, structural conditions that allow for interracial interactions, barriers between fostering interracial camaraderie, and campus cultures concerning cross-racial interactions. Diversity, then, might be understood as a process, with barriers and facilitators to beneficial diverse processes.

Usefully, some scholars conceptualize of diversity in more processual and relational terms. Ahmed (2007), recognizing the actors making up the diversity process, examines the experiences of diversity "workers" in a higher education context. Through the lens of critical race theory and settler colonialism frameworks, Patel (2015) also challenges the substantialist construction of diversity. Framing diversity as a desire, Patel argues that institutional actors desire the veneer of diversity without the necessary restructuring of university policies and practices that might facilitate a diverse population with equitable experiences. With this framing, she examines a central, often contradictory, relationship in diversity on college campuses—those who desire and the object of their desire (Patel 2015, 659). She identifies institutional agents and administrators as those who desire and underrepresented minorities as the objects of that desire.

Warikoo (2016), in another example, troubles the idea of diversity, adopting a more relational approach, examining how White students at elite institutions often view diversity as a bargain. Warikoo found that White students welcome efforts to diversify the racial demographics of campus because minorities expose Whites to diverse cultures and perspectives, thereby helping White students become more cosmopolitan. As long as White students benefit from a more cosmopolitan experience and are not academically threatened by racial minorities, Warikoo argues, diversity is welcomed. This approach is more processual in nature in that Warikoo constructs diversity as a continuous transaction.

Using a relational lens to understand diversity is beneficial both practically and scholastically. When administrators and school leaders understand diversity as a never-ending, dynamic process as opposed to a magic number to be achieved, their practices and policies might likewise evolve. Furthermore, rather than viewing diversity as an end goal existing in a hopeful future, a relational lens compels campus stakeholders to engage with their own active influence in diversity on campus.

Informed by relational sociology, scholars might endeavor to learn what structural and cultural conditions facilitate positive cross-racial interactions in a particular institutional context. A relational perspective pushes one to consider how the objective percentages and programs shape meso- and micro-interactions (Emirbayer 1997). In other words, given the objective numbers of students and resources given to ethnic-specific organizations at an institution, for example, how (if at all) are students of different races interacting?

From Racial Slights to Racialized Transactions

Race relations research in higher education often highlights or alludes to faculty and student experiences with microaggressions (e.g., Yosso et al. 2009). Chester Pierce, a psychologist, first coined the term to describe "subtle, stunning, often automatic and nonverbal exchanges which are 'put-downs' of blacks by offenders" (Pierce, Carew, Pierce-Gonzalez, & Willis 1978, 66). The phrase has since been used by higher education scholars as an analytic tool to describe the verbal and nonverbal implicit racialized insults incurred by underrepresented racial minorities (see Solórzano et al. 2000).

The microaggressions research project, however, is under increased scrutiny. A central criticism of microaggressions research is that racial minorities are sometimes characterized in a homogeneous manner (Lilienfeld 2017). Lilienfeld, for example, stated that microaggressions research "largely overlooks the possibility—indeed, the probability—that individual differences color recipients' interpretations of, and reactions to, microaggressions" (2017, 159). In responding to Lilienfeld's (2017) critique, Sue called up the African proverb, "Until the lions have their story tellers, stories of the hunt will always glorify the hunter." He suggested that he was viewing the issue of microaggressions from the lion's perspective and Lilienfeld viewing the issue from the hunter's perspective (Sue 2017). As a rejoinder to this response, Lilienfeld retorted that the lived reality of non-White individuals was not in question, rather, "the question is how best to construe this reality" (2017, 179).

This reality might be better construed in a relational sense. Using the same African proverb Sue invoked, one might consider how Dewey and Bentley construe hunting as a relationship (as cited by Emirbayer 1997, 289). Hunting, they argue, is impossible to understand without referencing the hunter, the hunted, and the relationship between them. Using Dewey and Bentley's example, we might construct the reality of microaggressions in a similar, relational sense. Microaggressions do not exist outside of the context and the various actors involved. Furthermore, the victim/receiver of a microaggression or the deliverer of a microaggression cannot be fully understood when analyzed as isolated entities.

Consider a brief scenario. One person says to a Black man who just presented in class, "You're so articulate." Depending on whom the statement comes from as well as the background of the Black man, the sentence might be received as a compliment or a microaggression. Microaggressions arise from internalized and relational features. Whether the encounter in question is understood as a microaggression is contingent on the relationship between the parties. For example, if the sentence comes from a close friend, he might take it as a compliment. If the statement comes from a non-Black student with whom he is not close, he might understand the words as a microaggression. Racialized thoughts about stereotypes of Black men might come to the presenter's mind in this scenario: "Were you surprised that I am articulate? Are you suggesting that most Black men are not articulate?" Depending on the presenter's upbringing, racial awareness, and personality however, he might simply take the words as a compliment regardless of who says them. Thus, microaggressions also have an internalized, individual component.

Rather than objective substances, some scholars construe microaggressions as components of social contexts and relationships (e.g., Douglass, Mirpuri, English, & Yip 2015; Ong, Fuller-Rowell, & Burrow 2009). Focusing the relational nature of racial slights, Douglass and colleagues (2015) examined how adolescents understood racist jokes among their friends. In another example, scholars studied racial distress not as an instance but longitudinally as a stress process (Ong et al. 2009).

Although not necessarily in name, some work has similarly identified the substantialist approach researchers have adopted in studying microaggressions. Ong and Burrow in reference to the construction of microaggressions in much of the literature, called for a "move beyond static representations of individuals to dynamic frameworks that observe people's lives as they unfold day to day" (2017, 173). While microaggressions research has certainly provided more insight into the subtle ways racism is imbued in some interactions and influences students' campus experiences, the concept of microaggressions might be better conceived with relational sociology in mind. In sum, by moving from diverse identities to diverse processes, atomized individuals to members of groups, and racial slights to racialized transactions, scholars might better engage with the relational nature of campus racial climate.

Conclusion

Campus racial climates, while thought to be multidimensional, are studied as if they are static, one-dimensional substances. Most campus climate research is similar—scholars examine how one preconstructed group perceives the climate (see Hurtado et al. 2008). Relational sociology provides a theoretical orientation for asking new questions, identifying new objects of analysis, and engaging with the multidimensional and intrinsically relational nature of the campus racial climate. At present, much campus climate literature tells us little more than who are the victims and who are the beneficiaries. This is a start.

Students experiencing negative racial climates deserve more than recitations of what they already know to be true about their campuses. The scholar's job is to illuminate truths using sophisticated theory and methods that might not otherwise be accessible. By engaging with the relational manner of racial life on campus, relational sociology provides new directions for race relations research and, more important, might yield pragmatic findings addressing race relations as a social problem and a very real aspect of life. The relational sociologist understands that the relationships shaping the qualities of campus racial climates can be reproduced or transformed. By identifying and studying relations and processes that facilitate or inhibit equitable campus experiences, a relational perspective sheds light on avenues for positive change. In relational sociology, scholars will find the analytic tools necessary to ask new questions, produce novel findings, and, in time, aid in transforming relationships that will facilitate more equitable campus racial climates for students of all races.

References

Ahmed, S. (2007). The language of diversity. *Ethnic and Racial Studies, 30*(2), 235–56.

Ahmed, S., & Swann, E. (2006). Doing diversity. *Policy Futures in Education, 42*(2), 96–100.

Allen, W. R., Epps, E. G., & Haniff, N. Z. (Eds). (1991). *College in Black and White: African American students in predominantly White and in historically Black public universities.* Albany, NY: State University of New York Press.

Boelens, R., Voet, M., & De Wever, B. (2018). The design of blended learning in response to student diversity in higher education: Instructors' views and use of differentiated instruction in blended learning. *Computers & Education, 120*, 197–212.

Bowman, N. A., & Park, J. J. (2014). Interracial contact on college campuses: Comparing and contrasting predictors of cross-racial interaction and interracial friendship. *Journal of Higher Education*, *85*(5), 660–90.

Cabrera, A. F., Nora, A., Terenzini, P. T., Pascarella, E., & Hagedorn, L. S. (1999). Campus racial climate and the adjustment of students to college: A comparison between White students and African-American students. *Journal of Higher Education*, *70*(2), 134–60.

Clarke, C. G., & antonio, a. l. (2012). Rethinking research on the impact of racial diversity in higher education. *Review of Higher Education*, *36*(1), 25–50.

Dépelteau, F. (2015). Relational sociology, pragmatism, transactions and social fields. *International Review of Sociology*, *25*(1), 45–64.

Desmond, M. (2012). Eviction and the reproduction of urban poverty. *American Journal of Sociology*, *118*(1), 88–133.

Desmond, M. (2014). Relational ethnography. *Theory and Society*, *43*(5), 547–79.

Dewey, J. (2008). Experience and nature. In *The later works of John Dewey, 1925–1953*, edited by J. Boydston & S. Hook, vol. 1, 1–437. 1925; Carbondale, IL: Southern Illinois University Press.

Dewey, J., & Bentley, A. F. (1960). *Knowing and the known*. Boston, MA: Beacon Press.

Douglass, S., Mirpuri, S., English, D., & Yip, T. (2015). "They were just making jokes": Ethnic/racial teasing and discrimination among adolescents. *Cultural Diversity & Ethnic Minority Psychology*, *22*, 69–82.

Du Bois, W. E. B. (1996). *The Philadelphia Negro: A social study*. 1899; Philadelphia, PA: University of Pennsylvania Press.

Elias, N. (1978) *What is sociology?*, translated by Stephen Mennell and Grace Morrissey. New York, NY: Columbia University Press.

Emirbayer, M. (1996). Useful Durkheim. *Sociological Theory*, *14*(2), 109–30.

Emirbayer, M. (1997). Manifesto for a relational sociology. *American Journal of Sociology*, *103*(2), 281–317.

Emirbayer, M., & Desmond, M. (2015). *The racial order*. Chicago, IL: University of Chicago Press.

Frazier, E. F. (1968). *E. Franklin Frazier on race relations*, edited by G. Edwards. Chicago, IL: University of Chicago Press.

Gurin, P., Dey, E., Hurtado, S., & Gurin, G. (2002). Diversity and higher education: Theory and impact on educational outcomes. *Harvard Educational Review*, *72*(3), 330–67.

Hall, R., & Sandler, B. (1982). The classroom climate: A chilly one for women. Washington, DC: Project in the Status and Education of Women, Association of American Colleges. Retrieved from https://files-eric-ed-gov.libproxy2.usc.edu/fulltext/ED254125.pdf.

Harper, S. R. (2012). Race without racism: How higher education researchers minimize racist institutional norms. *Review of Higher Education*, *36*(1), 9–29.

Harper, S., & Davis C.H.F., III. (2017, August 12). What UVA did wrong when white supremacists came to campus. *Los Angeles Times.* Retrieved from http://www.latimes.com/opinion/op-ed/la-oe-harper-davis-uva-white-supremacists-20170812-story.html.

Harper, S. R., & Hurtado, S. (2007). Nine themes in campus racial climates and implications for institutional transformation. *New Directions for Student Services, 120*, 7–24.

Harwood, S. A., Huntt, M. B., Mendenhall, R., & Lewis, J. A. (2012). Racial microaggressions in the residence halls: Experiences of students of color at a predominantly White university. *Journal of Diversity in Higher Education, 5*(3), 159.

Hurtado, S. (1992). The campus racial climate: Contexts of conflict. *Journal of Higher Education, 63*(5), 539–69.

Hurtado, S., Clayton-Pedersen, A. R., Allen, W. R., & Milem, J. F. (1998). Enhancing campus climates for racial/ethnic diversity: Educational policy and practice. *Review of Higher Education, 21*(3), 279–302.

Hurtado, S., Griffin, K. A., Arellano, L., & Cuellar, M. (2008). Assessing the value of climate assessments: Progress and future directions. *Journal of Diversity in Higher Education, 1*, 204–21.

Ignatiev, N. (2012). *How the Irish became White.* New York, NY: Routledge.

Jackson, J. L. (2001). *Harlemworld: Doing race and class in contemporary Black America.* Chicago, IL: University of Chicago Press.

Kim, C. J. (1999). The racial triangulation of Asian Americans. *Politics & Society, 27*(1), 105–38.

Lilienfeld, S. O. (2017). Microaggressions: Strong claims, inadequate evidence. *Perspectives on Psychological Science, 12*(1), 138–69.

Liu, S., & Emirbayer, M. (2016). Field and ecology. *Sociological Theory, 34*(1), 62–79.

Neuman, S. (2017, August 19). Duke University removes Robert E. Lee statue from chapel entrance. *NPR: The Two-Way.* Retrieved from https://www.npr.org/sections/thetwo-way/2017/08/19/544678037/duke-university-removes-robert-e-lee-statue-from-chapel-entrance.

Nuñez, A.-M. (2009). Latino students' transitions to college: A social and intercultural capital perspective. *Harvard Educational Review, 79*(1), 22–48.

Omi, M., & Winant, H. (2014). *Racial formation in the United States.* New York, NY: Routledge.

Ong, A. D., & Burrow, A. L. (2017). Microaggressions and daily experience: Depicting life as it is lived. *Perspectives on Psychological Science, 12*(1), 173–75.

Ong, A. D., Fuller-Rowell, T., & Burrow, A. L. (2009). Racial discrimination and the stress process. *Journal of Personality and Social Psychology, 96*, 1259–71.

Park, J. J. (2009). Are we satisfied? A look at student satisfaction with diversity at traditionally white institutions. *Review of Higher Education, 32*(3), 291–20.

Park, J. J. (2014). Clubs and the campus racial climate: Student organizations and interracial friendship in college. *Journal of College Student Development, 55*(7), 641–60.

Park, J. J., & Kim, Y. K. (2013). Interracial friendship and structural diversity: Trends for Greek, religious, and ethnic student organizations. *Review of Higher Education, 37*(1), 1–24.

Patel, L. (2015). Desiring diversity and backlash: White property rights in higher education. *Urban Review, 47*(4), 657–75.

Patton, L. D. (2016). Disrupting postsecondary prose: Toward a critical race theory of higher education. *Urban Education, 51*(3), 315–42.

Pierce, C., Carew, J., Pierce-Gonzalez, D., & Willis, D. (1978). An experiment in racism: TV commercials. In *Television and education*, edited by C. Pierce, 62–88. Beverly Hills, CA: Sage.

Racial tension and protests on campuses across the country. (2015, November 10). *New York Times*. Retrieved from https://www.nytimes.com/2015/11/11/us/racial-tension-and-protests-on-campuses-across-the-country.html.

Ray, V. E., Randolph, A., Underhill, M., & Luke, D. (2017). Critical race theory, Afro-pessimism, and racial progress narratives. *Sociology of Race and Ethnicity, 3*(2), 147–58.

Rediker, M. (2007). *The slave ship: A human history*. New York, NY: Penguin.

Smith, D. G. (2015). *Diversity's promise for higher education: Making it work*. Baltimore, MD: Johns Hopkins University Press.

Solórzano, D., Ceja, M., & Yosso, T. (2000). Critical race theory, racial microaggressions, and campus racial climate: The experiences of African American college students. *Journal of Negro Education, 69*(1), 60–73.

Stancill, J. (2017, September 23). UNC protest against Silent Sam now moving to campus store and restaurants. *News & Observer*. Retrieved from http://www.newsobserver.com/news/local/education/article174232166.html.

Sue, D. W. (2017). Microaggressions and "evidence": Empirical or experiential reality? *Perspectives on Psychological Science, 12*(1), 170–72.

Tichavakunda, A. A. (2017). Perceptions of financial aid: Black students at a predominantly White institution. *Educational Forum, 81*(1), 3–17.

Turner, C. S. V. (1994). Guests in someone else's house: Students of color. *Review of Higher Education, 17*(4), 355–70.

Warikoo, N. K. (2016). *The diversity bargain: And other dilemmas of race, admissions, and meritocracy at elite universities*. Chicago, IL: University of Chicago Press.

Yosso, T., Smith, W., Ceja, M., & Solórzano, D. (2009). Critical race theory, racial microaggressions, and campus racial climate for Latina/o undergraduates. *Harvard Educational Review, 79*(4), 659–91.

Chapter 5

Reconsidering the Role of College Advisors as Key Relationship Brokers in High School Networks

HOORI S. KALAMKARIAN, ANTHONY LISING ANTONIO, TAMARA GILKES BORR, AND JESSE FOSTER

Since the early debates of the classical theorists, sociologists have contemplated the role of structure versus agency for individuals within society. Education researchers also tend to work within this binary, often engaging a structuralist or agentic stance in their research. Although these approaches both have merit, a relational perspective allows for exploring the interplay between individual action and social forces. Research on college outreach programs from organizations outside the school (external college programs, ECPs) tends to focus on how actors, such as college counselors, affect postsecondary application rates and enrollment. A relational approach prompts us to look beyond individual outcomes.

To more fully understand the social space occupied by a set of actors in the social structure and how subjects engage agency in their relational position in that social space, we require a methodology that can capture the social structure, the set of relationships within that structure, and the meanings derived from those relationships simultaneously. For this reason, we propose a mixed-methods approach, combining network data collection with in-depth interviews to illuminate this important field of interaction. We develop the rationale for this specific method and provide an example of how it helps illuminate the ways different actors view and influence the social networks that affect college advising activities in schools.

Moving toward a Relational Framework in College Access Research

Structuralism, which cuts across many fields (such as sociology, anthropology, and education), emphasizes the role of society and assumes that individuals and their actions are constrained by the real bounds of the determinative social structure (Waters 1994). There are many examples of this framework in education, and a common implication of structuralist thinking is the prominence of substantialist variables typically used in quantitative analyses. Through this lens, groups of people are studied within their socially determined boundaries (e.g., race, gender, class).

An agentic perspective positions people as capable of acting intentionally. Much like structuralism, the concept of agency or methodological individualism cuts across many academic fields. Generally, however, "A stress on agency implies that individuals are not the products or even the victims of the social world but rather that they are thinking, feeling and acting subjects who create the world around them" (Waters 1994, 15). In education research privileging agency, students are studied as individual actors capable of making their own (often rational) choices.

Both approaches have value. However, as Kolluri and Tierney describe in chapter 1, a relational approach has emerged in sociology that eschews the agency-structure dichotomy. As stated by Mustafa Emirbayer, "Relational theorists reject the notion that one can posit discrete, pre-given units such as the individual or society as ultimate starting points of sociological analysis. . . . Individual persons, whether strategic or norm following, are inseparable from the transactional contexts within which they are embedded" (Emirbayer 1997, 287). Studying the individual and society is valuable, but the bulk of education research has tended to ignore this inseparable quality, potentially overstating the preeminence of one or the other. As such, we embrace a relational perspective that focuses on the ties between actors and the meanings people bring to and derive from those relationships.

Capturing the relationships that lie somewhere between the individual and the social structure requires an innovative set of methods. Claude Lévi-Strauss posited that the social structure is unknown to individual people, despite them being unconsciously constrained by it (Waters 1994). Overall, if social structure is unknown to an individual, methods used to investigate this structure must account for this invisibility. However, if people make meaning despite not fully perceiving this structure, then our method must also capture this individual rationalization. According to Pierre Bourdieu (1988), a relational method devoid of capturing the hierarchies entrenched in power and fights for capital is insufficient. A mixed-methods approach is capable of capturing these intricacies, if employed appropriately.

To capture the invisible social structure, we use network analysis. By gathering data from individuals about their relationships, we can draw conclusions about the social structure that may be unknown to an individual actor. To capture the meaning of interactions in these relationships, we use in-depth interviews. Although these interviews may not provide insight into the elements of the social structure unknown to the individual actors, they do provide insight into the rationalization and meaning-making of the actor. By strategically interviewing participants throughout various parts of the network, we gain insight into the structure of power relations from the viewpoint of the actors. Coupled with the network data, our mixed-methods relational approach has the potential to provide a deeper understanding of how ECPs embedded in high schools affect advising practices beyond their own.

College advising within high schools is an inherently relational phenomenon. Parents and students receive information directly from the college advisor. Teachers, counselors, and other school staff provide information to advisors about the students, and advisors provide information about college-going processes with school staff. Parents and students discuss their desires and aspirations with each other and the high school teachers, counselors, and advisors. Thus, research that focuses only on the parameters of the social structure or the actions of an individual—thereby ignoring the central practice of advising—is ill-equipped to capture the relational contexts and activity that codetermine the specific character of these consequential advising structures and practices. As such, we use a relational approach to analyze practices of information sharing in high schools and illuminate how ECP advisors and school staff forge channels of communication and develop networks of cooperation.

The Role of External College Programs

Efforts to improve higher education attainment, particularly among underrepresented subgroups, increasingly include investment in college outreach programs that provide supplementary college preparation and advising services to schools (College Board 1999; Swail & Perna 2002). Although ECPs are increasingly popular, knowledge of what these programs provide and their effectiveness in raising college-going rates is limited. Studies of ECPs find, at best, modest gains in postsecondary enrollment for participating students (Bergin, Cooks, & Bergin 2007; Constantine, Seftor, Martine, Silva, & Myers 2006; Domina 2009; Maxfield, Schirm, & Rodriguez-Planas 2003). The modest effects on student outcomes, however, do not offer a complete picture of how programs may contribute to college readiness and higher education access. In addition to directly serving students, ECPs may catalyze changes in school practices that affect students' academic preparedness and postsecondary trajectories.

Several programs are increasingly articulating explicit goals around motivating systemic, school-level change and adopting school-wide outreach efforts instead of targeting specific students (Domina 2009). Moreover, the school-based structure of a large proportion of programs suggests that programs may be in a position to shape school-level practices. At least one study has documented spillover effects of such programs on nonparticipants (Domina 2009), presumably driven by interaction between programs and schools that result in changes to school practices, approaches, and outlooks toward postsecondary advising and preparation.

The indirect effect ECPs have on school practices may be a more authentic representation of the way programs can move the needle on academic performance and postsecondary outcomes for students. These outcomes are the product of complex school processes, including classroom instruction and the expectations for students around college and career preparation (McDonough 2005; Roderick, Nagaoka, Coca, & Moeller 2008). In their reviews and analyses of program evaluations, Swail and Perna (2000), Gándara (2001), Gullatt and Jan (2003), and Schultz and Mueller (2006) all identify this systemic role for ECPs as an important but understudied function. Gullatt and Jan suggest that integrating programs with school functions likely positions programs to "marry their interests" (2003, 14) with the objectives espoused by schools and thereby bolster school practices around college readiness.

Evaluation studies suggest that information from ECPs may inform how school staff approach college preparation and advising. ECPs, in emulating the approach college-prep academies take to college preparation, facilitate entry and diffusion of new information about college in schools. This includes maintaining up-to-date and specialized information about colleges to guide students through the search and application cycle (Gándara 2001; Standing, Judkins, Keller, & Shimshak 2008). Teachers, counselors, and principals shape students' postsecondary trajectories not only through academic training but also in terms of the way and extent to which they discuss college and the postsecondary expectations they uphold (McDonough 2005; Roderick et al. 2008). Through information sharing, external programs can significantly shape these practices.

Moving toward a Relational Understanding of External College Programs

Prior research on the role of ECPs focuses on individual student outcomes and the role of these programs in broader organizational practices at the school level. However, the nature of these external programs, serving as sources of information to stakeholders in the school and other external programs in the same building, suggests the need for a relational framework.

A dominant thread in the field of organizational studies defines knowledge sharing as the precursor to organizational learning (Borgatti & Foster, 2003; Ipe, 2003; Simon, 1991; Tsai, 2001). More specifically, interfirm knowledge sharing is necessary to facilitate organizational learning; knowledge transfer between different firms allows new knowledge to enter organizations and motivate innovation. An emerging literature suggests that this perspective may extend to schools. Schools are more likely to adopt reforms if the new practices are transmitted through relationships between staff colleagues (Daly 2010; Moolenaar, Daly, & Sleegers 2010). Several recent empirical studies investigating adoption and diffusion of innovative teaching practices validate this perspective. For example, in a mixed-methods study using a social network approach, Spillane, Hopkins, and Sweet (2015) mapped interactions among teachers within and between schools in two districts. They found that interaction with formally designated lead teachers was integral to the adoption and spread of instructional reforms. Similarly, Penuel, Riel, Krause, and Frank (2009) found that the relationship between novice and expert teachers explains the variation in the novice instructors' responsiveness to pedagogical reforms.

In the same way, the structure of social relations among school and ECP staff may explain how information about college possessed by external programs enters and is shared throughout schools. Furthermore, a relational approach posits that the meanings people derive from these information-sharing relations influence how and what kind of information is shared. By focusing on the relationships between actors, rather than just the individuals or the larger organization, a relational approach provides a perspective on the potential effectiveness of these programs that operates by reconfiguring the understandings and behaviors associated with college advising. We assume that the relations between programmatic actors and school actors form an in-school network within which knowledge is exchanged. We refer to this as the college information network. In what follows, we examine relations among school and external program staff and illustrate how interactions in the college information network reflect the interdependence of the structure of those relationships and the perceptions that each have regarding their involvement in college advising efforts in a school.

Methods and Data

We examine two cases of college information networks with a mixed-methods design. Congruent with a relational approach, we pursue a "complementarity" mixed-methods design (Greene, Caracelli, & Graham 1989), which allows for inquiry that uncovers the structure (via network analytic methods) and the meaning and context (via ethnographic interviews and observations) of the relations defined by participation in college information sharing. The inquiry has interpretive and positivist features. The comparative design provides case variation to illuminate theoretically relevant features in the information sharing relations within the schools.

Case Sampling

The cases analyzed here are drawn from a larger study of college advising practices in New York City. New York resembles many urban areas with a number of ECPs operating in the city. We partnered with one external provider, the College Advising Program[1] (CAP), to gain access to school sites and provide a consistent provider across cases. For the larger project, cases were selected with a maximum variation, 2 × 2 design. We selected cases to (1) vary the number of ECPs operating in schools (one versus multiple) and (2) provide variance in college-going culture. The latter was indicated by a New York Department of Education college and career readiness index.[2] The two cases we analyze here were at opposite ends of the college and career readiness index but maintained relationships with multiple ECPs (see table 5.1).

Table 5.1. Case selection data

School	Size	% Free and Reduced Lunch	% Black/ Hispanic	Graduation Rate (%)	College Enrollment Rate ($)	College/Career Readiness Index	External Programs in School
Union	~300	~90	~65	~80	50–70	Top quarter	CAP; Reach
Valley	~400	~85	~90	~60	20–40	Bottom quarter	CAP; College Ready; ServeNY; GRAD; NYC Cares

Note: School and external program names are pseudonyms.

Source: Hoori Kalamkarian.

Data Collection and Analysis

The first author was the primary researcher for data collection, conducted during the 2013–14 school year. For each school, we conducted three-day site visits with a two-person research team. Data collection included a network survey, semi-structured interviews, and observations of college advising activities. We used a survey to identify the network of school staff and ECP staff involved in college advising and interviews to reveal attitudes and approaches to advising and the nature of college-related interactions. We initiated data collection with an interview and survey administered to the CAP advisor. The CAP advisor was an important initiation point for two reasons. First, the program was common to both cases and allowed for some comparability of network identification. Second, the CAP advisor is a full-time presence, and in schools where most college advising is provided part-time and is often cohort-based, the CAP advisor is potentially a central figure. Using the survey, we collected a list of network alters by using a name generator asking respondents to identify "the people with whom you discuss matters related to college and career preparation." This list was used to identify additional informants to be interviewed and surveyed. Through this snowballing process, we interviewed and surveyed between ten and thirteen staff members in each school. Informants included administrators, teachers, counselors, and staff from ECPs working in schools.

Coding and analysis of the interview data were completed using Dedoose analytic software. The research team developed a coding scheme based on the models of collaboration and information sharing developed by Coburn and Russell (2008) and Dyer and Nobeoka (2000). We organized our codes into four broad thematic areas: context of interaction, content of interaction, directionality of the interaction, and type of knowledge shared. Analysis consisted of coding; fact-checking school features, policies, and practices; weekly research team discussions of emergent themes; and triangulation of themes and findings across informants, informant types, individual researchers, and colleagues familiar with the work of ECPs. We used STATA to identify each school's college information-sharing network and to calculate network and tie properties.

The Cases

Union High School

Union High School is a small, comprehensive high school located in lower Manhattan near New York City's Chinatown. Union serves approximately

331 students. A large majority of students are socioeconomically disadvantaged; approximately 85 percent receive free and reduced-price lunch. A large majority are also racial minorities, including African Americans, Latinos, and Asians. Stakeholders (all interviewees including school staff, students, parents, ECP staff) note the social and familial challenges that several Union students experience. One counselor characterized the student population as "single-parent homes, drugs, abuse—so much of that."

In recent years, as one counselor put it, the school has been "getting back on its feet." Administrators, teachers, counselors, and students described this transition as a shift in the school's norms and values. For example, one student sensed attention on "fixing" the school to create a "good environment for people to learn." Similarly, a counselor chronicled a shift in attention from disciplinary issues, such as fights and tardiness, to "focusing more on the end goal; instruction, college readiness, preparing these kids for the future." Amid this transition, college-going has emerged as the primary postsecondary pathway students are encouraged to pursue among the menu of options. One teacher described the emphasis on college as "a lot of demand placed on (students) to like, college, college, college." Students also identified such expectations in their school.

College advising is primarily the responsibility of the CAP advisor with the assistance of Reach, a local external outreach program that offers college, academic, and extracurricular supplementary programming. Both programs are present at the school on a full-time, daily basis. Union dedicates one classroom on the third floor as the college center, staffed by the CAP advisor and three Reach staff members. The CAP advisor and Reach staff have open workspaces adjacent to each other against the back wall of the room. Students frequently come through the college center between classes and during lunch periods for advising or simply to talk with the staff. The college center and the activities the staff sponsor are the primary resources for college preparation and advising at Union. The eleventh-/twelfth-grade counselor also contributes by helping students with their college applications and administering activities, such as a campus career fair.

Valley High School

Valley is among three public schools in a visually striking building with bright green, blue, and red framing. The building's modern, uplifting appearance sits in a neighborhood where, as one informant described, the "blocks are ridden with gang violence." Each year, the school hosts a school-wide March Against Violence rally in remembrance of two students who were killed by gun violence in 2008. The student population at Valley is composed almost entirely of students of color. Valley is small school, enrolling approximately 400 students.

Staff members and students described the school as an increasingly tense environment. For students, the tension manifested in terms of a strict administration and more frequent confrontations between students and school leadership around behavioral issues. For the adults, there was a palpable tension between the administration and the faculty. From the perspective of teachers, counselors, and external program staff, including the CAP advisor, the tense relationship was due to the administration's lack of vision. As one special education teacher noted, "As a staff—and because there's no clear vision—we don't know what our focus is. So it makes it really difficult to meet your goals if you don't know what the goal is."

College advising at Valley is formally structured as the responsibility of one full-time counselor and one part-time counselor, who also teaches science courses. The school also partners with several other ECPs with an on-site presence that provides college readiness and advising services. These programs vary in structure and scope. ServeNY, like the CAP advisor, has a full-time presence at Valley; one full-time and one part-time representative administer the organization's school-wide and cohort-specific service learning projects. GRAD, a federally funded college outreach program, has a part-time presence at Valley and works in the counseling center with a specific cohort of seniors. As part of the school's expeditionary learning model, Valley also partners with College Ready, a national nonprofit organization that promotes active learning and character building in and out of the classroom. Similarly, NYC Cares, a local nonprofit, facilitates college advising services through the part-time school counselor.

Despite these extensive partnerships, the data suggest that college-going was not uniformly treated as a high priority across staff members at Valley. Whereas most staff members want students to have "college and other life after high school options," as one teacher with administrative duties noted, there was a general feeling that the school as a whole did not do enough to talk about and prepare students for postsecondary opportunities. The varying characterizations of the school's college-going culture reflect the different expectations faculty and counselors expressed for students' postsecondary trajectories.

Findings

As stated already, a relational perspective is twofold. It involves understanding the social structure and the patterns of meaning-making among the actors. Our network data illuminate the social structure in our cases, highlighting the central role of the ECP staff. Meanwhile, our interview data illuminate how actors share information and the meaning they derive from these actions. Together, these data allow us to observe the structure of the network and provide an understanding of how each actor's perceptions and roles interplay with their structural position.

The Centrality of Advising: Insights from the Network Analysis

We display graphs of the college information networks in figures 5.1 and 5.2. All ties are directed, emanating from the nominating actor and

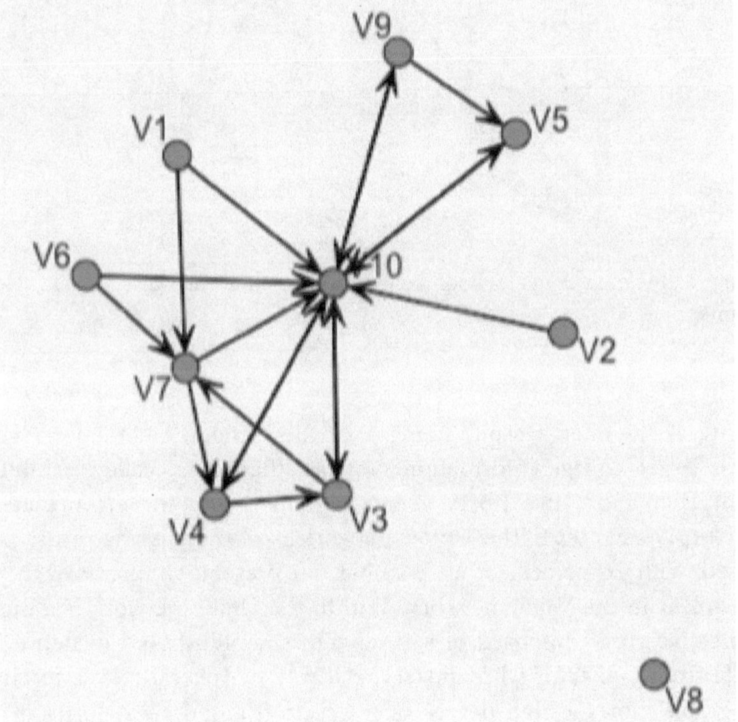

Figure 5.1. Valley High School college information network. *Source:* Hoori Kalamkarian.

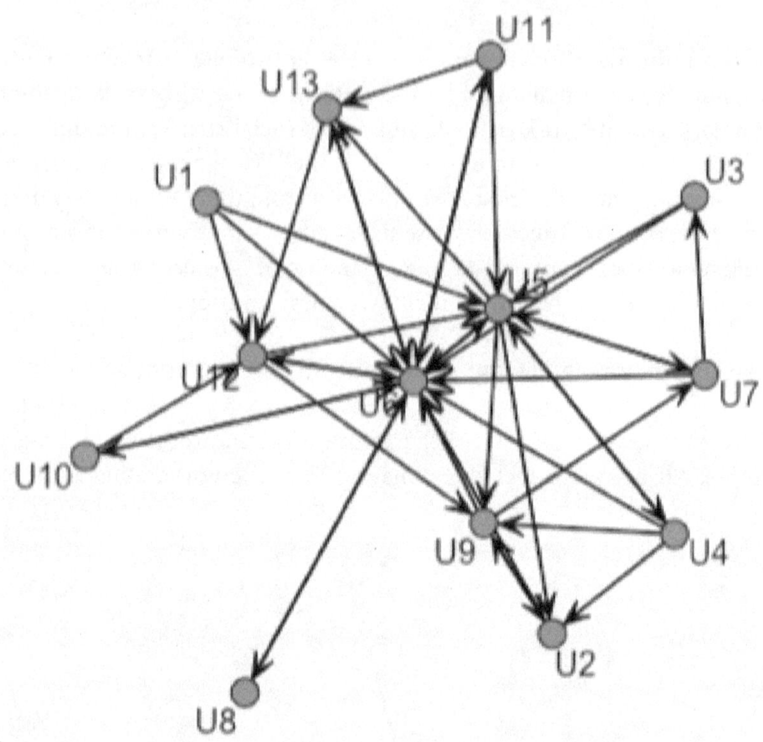

Figure 5.2. Union High School college information network. *Source:* Hoori Kalamkarian.

ending at the alter. Despite being a smaller school, Union possesses a much larger college information network than does Valley, exhibiting twenty-two more ties (forty versus eighteen) and three more actors (thirteen versus ten). The Union network is also somewhat more connected, with 26 percent of all possible ties present, compared with just 20 percent in the Valley network. Within the Union network is a highly connective core composed of several actors, as illustrated in figure 5.2. Aside from one actor who appears relatively peripheral (U8, a teacher), the graph shows a high degree of interaction among a majority of the actors. In the more sparse network at Valley, the CAP advisor (V10) is clearly the center of the network.

In both the Valley and Union college information networks, we find that stakeholders are generally positioned as would be expected given their job functions. This is illustrated structurally when examining measures of centrality (tables 5.2 and 5.3). Indegree, the count of ties directed to

Table 5.2. Actor centrality in Union Network

Actor	Function	Indegree Centrality	Betweenness Centrality
U6	CAP advisor	12	57.5
U5	11th/12th grade counselor	9	52.5
U9	Assistant principal	4	5.5
U12	Reach supervisor (full-time)	4	10.5
U13	Reach advisor (part-time)	3	1
U2	10th grade counselor	3	0
U7	Teacher	2	11
U8	Teacher	1	0
U10	Reach advisor (part-time)	1	0
U11	Teacher	1	0
U3	Teacher	1	0
U4	Teacher	1	12
U1	Teacher	0	0

Source: Hoori Kalamkarian.

Table 5.3. Actor centrality in Valley Network

Actor	Function	Indegree Centrality	Betweenness Centrality
V10	CAP advisor	8	26
V7	Counselor	3	1.5
V3	Teacher	2	5
V4	Instructional coach	2	0.5
V5	ServeNY staff (full-time)	2	0
V9	ServeNY staff (part-time)	1	0
V2	Teacher	0	0
V1	Assistant principal	0	0
V6	Teacher	0	0
V8	Teacher	0	0

Source: Hoori Kalamkarian.

an actor, is a measure of the relative centrality of an actor in a network (Wasserman & Faust 1994). In this context, greater indegree is indicative of a staff member who is more often sought out for providing or receiving information related to college. In both schools, the CAP advisor and one counselor are the most central actors. The betweenness centrality of an actor is the number of shortest paths between any two actors in the network that pass through that actor (Scott 2000). As defined, it is a measure of influence and control of information flow in the network, and again, the CAP advisor and the eleventh-/twelfth-grade counselor are dominant figures at Union. They serve as information brokers in the network (Burt 1992), a role we take up later in our analysis. At Valley, information sharing between other actors is almost exclusively mediated by the CAP advisor.

Staff from Reach are also central in the Union network, highlighted by U12, a full-time school-based representative of the program. The part-time staff of Reach (U10, U13), not surprisingly, are more peripheral in the network. Overall, the Reach staff are embedded in 33 percent of the observed ties with connections that span across administrators, counselors, teachers, and the CAP advisor. In contrast, the primary external partner for college advising beyond the CAP program at Valley, ServeNY, has staff that are peripherally positioned in the network. This is expected given that ServeNY is not exclusively focused on college preparation.

Teachers are generally peripheral in both networks, exhibiting low centrality from this structural perspective. Many more teachers participate in information sharing at Union than at Valley, where some degree of participation in college-related activities is expected of teachers. A few teachers are structurally exceptional in each school, occupying broker positions in their respective networks. For example, a special education teacher at Valley (V3) exhibits a relatively high betweenness centrality, and at Union, two illustrate betweenness of similar magnitude as the full-time Reach staff member.

Transmission and Collaboration in College Information Networks: Insights from the Qualitative Data

The network analysis allowed us to locate the structural position of actors, providing insight into their involvement in the college advising process. In both schools, the CAP advisor is structurally central and is illustrative of how an ECP enacts a primary role in college advising. However, insight into how such a role may affect school practices is not easily discernible. In this section, we provide additional perspective with an analysis of interview data to show how college information is shared in those networks.

Stakeholders engage in various ways to share knowledge in college information networks. Two of the most common types of interactions illustrate distinct practices: transmission and collaboration. At Union and Valley, stakeholders disseminate explicit or "easily codifiable" (Dyer & Nobeoka 2000, 5) information about the college search and application process, such as facts about various postsecondary institutions. Such interactions function as transmission activities where updates or facts related to postsecondary pathways are passed to other actors. Moreover, the transmission of explicit information almost exclusively originates from school and ECP staff positioned as brokers. For example, the Valley CAP advisor manages a Google document tracking each senior's status on several components of the application process, including financial aid form completion, submission of letters of recommendation, and application status. The document is used to transmit updates about the senior class to instructors, administrators, counselors, and other program staff. Staff describe the document as being "for viewing purposes" and "to see where our kids were" in terms of the college application process.

In contrast, collaborative activities involve greater engagement between two actors. We construe collaboration as a "joint venture" (Gulati, Wohlgezogen, & Zhelyazkov 2012, 3) where individuals pool their resources and expertise to solve a common problem (Phillips, Lawrence, & Hardy 2000). Consequently, collaboration is a cognitive engagement that may draw on tacit knowledge (less tangible information, such as personal experiences or heuristics) and explicit knowledge (Dyer & Nobeoka 2000; Finnigan, Daly, & Che 2012; Philips et al. 2000; Trist 1983).

Collaborative interactions are present in both networks but are comparatively limited at Valley. Various Valley informants described the CAP advisor's practices as including consultation with stakeholders across the school. For example, a ServeNY staff member told us of a typical interaction where "she'll come asking us about what's going on with a student" and then they will work together to determine how to support the student's postsecondary plans, such as brainstorming financial aid strategies for a senior who needed an additional $12,000 to pay for private school.

This type of "tag team" (as the ServeNY informant called it) appears to primarily occur between the CAP advisor and ServeNY staff. These interactions are almost exclusively initiated by the advisor, who is structurally positioned as a broker. On the other hand, we find a wide range of responses to efforts by the CAP advisor to engage teachers in college advising. The Valley CAP advisor explained:

> Some of them were super responsive . . . and would stop by and meet with me frequently. So [one teacher], would email or meet with me pretty often to know the specifics of where each member of her crew was at and what support she could offer. Others were totally unresponsive to emails.

This range is especially evident in the CAP advisor's description of her colleagues' response to the Google document to track each senior's progress on college applications and related items. Describing the use of the document, the CAP advisor said some "never look at it even once," whereas others "took a consistent interest."

In contrast, collaborative interactions are common at Union, especially between the centrally positioned staff. For example, the CAP advisor, eleventh-/twelfth-grade counselor, and Reach supervisor all described consulting one another when working with particular students on college applications. The Reach supervisor noted that he and the CAP advisor are constantly sharing ideas and "figuring out" how to advise students or what services to offer.

At Union, the CAP advisor and other program staff positioned as brokers also initiate collaborative interactions with many teachers, who again are peripherally positioned in the network. For example, all teachers in the network across grade levels participated in preparing for and executing the college fair organized by the CAP advisor and Reach staff. In planning for the fair, the staff discussed the event at an all-staff meeting. As one teacher noted, these discussions served as opportunities for various teachers to share their ideas for the day: "[Teacher A] was the one who had said, 'Oh, we should wear our college shirts.' She's the math teacher. And then since I wasn't here last year, [teacher B] was saying what kinds of things they did last year, and like what worked, what didn't work." According to various informants, the feedback from instructors who had previously experienced the fair was especially useful as the staff deliberated various strategies for facilitating conversations between students and fair facilitators. At Union, the CAP advisor, Reach supervisor, and other broker actors consulted with teachers individually and jointly through email when advising students on college options and designing SAT workshops and other supplementary academic programs.

In general, our interview data clarify that different types of knowledge are shared in college information networks. The interview data coupled with the network data provide deeper insight. Through this combined analysis, it is clear that knowledge sharing is cultivated and pursued by broker actors, and significantly, those brokers are often ECP staff. Furthermore, we learn that Union's network is comparatively rich in collaborative relations that leverage the knowledge of peripherally positioned actors.

Relationships and Trajectories of Action

Informants' perceptions of their role in the network offer some insight into the differences in information-sharing relationships we observe between the school sites. At Union, through her relationships with teachers, the CAP advisor envisions and enacts her role as one that collaborates with school staff. At the start of her tenure at the school, the advisor described interacting with teachers "just to introduce myself." Following a workshop she facilitated on writing effective letters of recommendation, however, the advisor's relationships recast the scope of her advising activities to include more collaborative interactions with teachers. She described how teachers "got to know me really more. And then they ask me questions on like recommendation letters. And from then on they just ask me, you know, 'Is she on top of the college application process?' or 'How does the common app work?' Things like that." What began as a relationship characterized by the advisor's practice of transmission (a workshop) evolved into one where collaborative advising practices are normative. In contrast, Valley's CAP advisor understands her role primarily as an accessible transmitter of information about college to students and staff. As she says, her main function is serving as "one central place that is there all the time for college information." This characterization appears to be informed by the specific nature of her relationship with teachers. She noted that very few teachers approach her for college materials or information; among those that do, their requests are limited to having her speak in their classes about the academic requirements for college admission.

We observe a similar link between teacher–advisor relations and the reach of teacher involvement in college advising. Teachers generally felt limited in their college advising abilities, often citing a key contextual feature of their relationship with the CAP advisor as a factor in this understanding, a disparity in college knowledge: "As teachers we don't necessarily have that degree of knowledge in colleges that [advisors] have" (Union teacher). The consequence for this teacher is that, because his college experience is local, he limits the content of his advising to information about local colleges. Outside of this narrow geographic scope, he cedes expertise to the CAP advisor. This demarcation was also evident at Valley, for example, when a teacher highlighted the CAP advisor's specialized knowledge in areas such as financial aid and expressed reliance on the advisor's guidance in supporting her students.

Although teachers from both schools emphasized their limitations when describing their college advising activities, teachers at Union exhibit more extensive involvement than their Valley counterparts. Union teachers described collaborative interactions with ECP staff, typically around sharing knowledge of students. For example, a teacher who lacked knowledge of specific postsecondary programs or institutions described their role in helping ECP staff get an accurate understanding of students' academic skills and likelihood of succeeding in different postsecondary contexts. From the teacher's perspective, "Because [the Reach supervisor] knows about their financial issues and everything and I know about their academic ability, we'll talk about it and try to collaborate on what schools are actually legitimate options for them." Awareness of their complementary knowledge helps define the nature of their collaboration. In contrast, several teachers at Valley expressed a commitment to supporting students' postsecondary enrollment and success, but they understood their contribution as limited to instruction and classroom mentions of college. For example, a teacher described occasionally "checking in" with the CAP advisor and asking questions like, "What can I do in the classroom? What can I talk to them about? What should I write in their transition plans?" Recall that Valley teachers described much fewer collaborative interactions than did their peers at Union, congruent with this more limited outlook on their involvement in college advising.

In these two school contexts, ECP advisors enacted their roles as college counselors differently. At Union, advisors were more often able to engage in collaborative interactions while also transmitting explicit information. At Valley, counselor actions were largely limited to giving out explicit information, and teachers were less active in their contributions to college advising. In each context, actors' college-advising activities appeared to be related not only to their structural position in the information sharing network but also, importantly, to their understandings of the reach and limits of their role that they derived through their relationships.

Lessons Learned from a Relational Approach

We argue that prior education research tends to adopt either a structuralist approach, emphasizing the role of society on the individual, or an individualistic stance, highlighting the agentic choices of the person. Together with the other authors in this book, we argue for a relational approach to education research that explores the interactions and meaning-making of people within the social spaces they inhabit. Education is an inherently relational phenomenon and thus requires relational methods to explore it. College advising is particularly relational; information exchange and consultation occurs among and between students, college counselors, teachers, and other stakeholders. Therefore, a relational method is particularly salient in this setting.

To understand how subjects embody agency within their relational position in a social space, we used a methodology that captured the social structure, the set of relationships in that structure, and the meanings derived from those relationships. We combined network data with in-depth interviews to analyze the interplay between structure and action and illuminate how different actors view and influence the social networks from which college advising practices emerge.

By engaging a relational perspective, we can examine external college programs embedded within their schooling context, an aspect missed by prior studies focusing solely on student outcomes. Structurally, we can recognize the prominent and important role played by an ECP staff (the CAP advisor) and one regular school staff member (a counselor). They are the figurative and literal center around college advising activities; others involved in this school effort are peripheral. However, this structural view obscures individual action that both belies and informs their structural position in the network. Moving between individual and network units of analysis, we now understand how teachers and the ECP advisors in these schools enact advising practices in ways that make sense in their relational contexts. In particular, the interview data allow us to see that the nature of the knowledge shared between central and peripheral actors varies across the two networks. While knowledge sharing is largely limited to transmitting explicit or factual information about the college search and application process at Valley, we observe more widespread collaborative engagement between ECP staff, counselors, and instructors at Union.

The agency of teachers and the CAP advisor—illustrated by the actions they undertake and understand to be within their purview as contributors to college advising—differ at the two schools because the relational context in which they are embedded also differs. At Union, the CAP advisor more often appropriates network connections and feels appropriately empowered to call on teachers to assist with activities such as college fairs and on counseling staff to jointly address student advising issues. The contrast with advising practices at Valley is striking, given a similarly structured college information network and a presumably identical job description for their CAP advisor.

As Ferrare argues in chapter 2 of this volume, understanding local action requires us to link "interdependent social relations to the perceptions that shape how actors interpret trajectories of action." The different relationships between school staff and the CAP advisors at Union and Valley point to at least one way an ECP can contribute to changes in school practices. In cocreating the college information network with school staff, they are partners to an evolution of practices that may include and normalize new relations of collaboration. The Valley case serves as a cautionary tale, however, underscoring how relational context matters for the development of networks that may (or may not) enhance functioning as is hoped for or intended. Moreover, the differences in teacher and advisor relations we encountered suggest the importance of identifying additional factors that may shape the relational context of schools, such as institutional norms, class and meeting schedules, and even the physical layout of the school (Kalamkarian 2016).

As other contributors in this volume also argue, employing a relational perspective in education research has the potential to uncover important aspects of educational practice. The move beyond a purely structural stance or an individualist approach to our scholarship affords a perspective with fewer (or at least smaller) conceptual and empirical blind spots in our work. The research presented in this chapter potentially yield policy and practice implications that may not surface with traditional methods. A network-based implication may point toward attention to the establishment of formal and informal connections between ECP and school staff. An agentic-based implication may focus on the need to ensure that teachers are involved in sharing information. A relational approach allows for the recognition of both sets of implications as well as a vital third one:

the context for information-sharing relationships should be one where collaboration is encouraged and expected, and where mutual recognition and valuation of specialized knowledges and information of teachers, counselors, and ECP staff is the norm. We recognize that additional blind spots are present in the current study, but the potential of a relational approach to enlarge our view of educational practices in schools begins to emerge in this work.

Notes

1. This and the names of all college access programs are pseudonyms.

2. The college and career readiness indicator is a composite of cohort-based measures of postsecondary enrollment, college prep curricula completion, regents diploma attainment, and college persistence one year after high school.

References

Bergin, D. A., Cooks, H. C., & Bergin, C.C. (2007). Effects of a college access program for youth underrepresented in higher education: A randomized experiment. *Research in Higher Education*, *48*(6), 727–50.

Borgatti, S. P., & Foster, P. C. (2003). The network paradigm in organizational research: A review and typology. *Journal of Management*, *29*(6), 991–1013.

Bourdieu, P. (1988). *Homo academicus*. Stanford, CA: Stanford University Press.

Burt, R. S. (1992). *Structural holes*. Cambridge, MA: Harvard University Press.

Coburn, C. E., & Russell, J. L. (2008). District policy and teachers' social networks. *Educational Evaluation and Policy Analysis*, *30*(3), 203–35.

College Board. (1999). *Trends in student aid 1999*. New York, NY: College Board.

Constantine, J. M., Seftor, N. S., Martine, E. S., Silva, T., & Myers, D. (2006). *A study of the effect of the talent search program on secondary and postsecondary outcomes in Florida, Indiana and Texas*. Washington, DC: US Department of Education.

Daly, A. J. (2010). *Social network theory and educational change*. Cambridge, MA: Harvard Education Press.

Domina, T. (2009). What works in college outreach: Assessing targeted and school wide interventions for disadvantaged students. *Educational Evaluation and Policy Analysis*, *31*(2), 127–52.

Dyer, J. H., & Nobeoka, K. (2000). Creating and managing a high-performance knowledge-sharing network: The Toyota case. *Strategic Management Journal*, *21*(3), 345–67.

Emirbayer, M. (1997). Manifesto for a relational sociology. *American Journal of Sociology, 103*(2), 281–317.

Finnigan, K., Daly, A., & Che, J. (2012). The acquisition and use of evidence district-wide. In *Annual Meeting of the American Educational Research Association, Vancouver, Canada*. Retrieved from http://www.wtgrantfoundation.org/resources/studying-the-use-of-research-evidence.

Gándara, P. (2001). *Paving the way to postsecondary education: K–12 intervention programs for underrepresented youth*. Report of the National Postsecondary Education Cooperative Working Group on Access to Postsecondary Education.

Greene, J. C., Caracelli, V. J., & Graham, W. F. (1989). Toward a conceptual framework for mixed-method evaluation designs. *Educational Evaluation and Policy Analysis, 11*(3), 255–74.

Gulati, R., Wohlgezogen, F., & Zhelyazkov, P. (2012). The two facets of collaboration: Cooperation and coordination in strategic alliances. *Academy of Management Annals, 6*, 531–83.

Gullatt, Y., & Jan, W. (2003). *How do pre-collegiate academic outreach programs impact college-going among underrepresented students*? Washington, DC: Pathways to College Network Clearinghouse.

Ipe, M. (2003). Knowledge sharing in organizations: A conceptual framework. *Human Resource Development Review, 2*(4), 337–59.

Kalamkarian, H. S. (2016). *Brokering information sharing: A social network perspective on school partnerships with college outreach programs*. PhD diss., Stanford University.

Maxfield, M., Schirm, A., & Rodriguez-Planas, N. (2003). *The Quantum Opportunity Program demonstration: Implementation and short-term impacts*. Mathematica Policy Research Report 8279-093. Washington, DC: Mathematica Policy Research.

McDonough, P. M. (2005). Counseling matters: Knowledge, assistance, and organizational commitment in college preparation. In *Preparing for college: Nine elements of effective outreach*, edited by W. G. Tierney, Z. B. Corwin, & J. E. Colyar, 69–87. Albany, NY: State University of New York Press.

Moolenaar, N. M., Daly, A. J., & Sleegers, P. J. C. (2010). Occupying the principal position: Examining relationships between transformational leadership, social network position, and schools' innovative climate. *Educational Administration Quarterly, 46*(5), 623–70.

Penuel, W., Riel, M., Krause, A., & Frank, K. (2009). Analyzing teachers' professional interactions in a school as social capital: A social network approach. *Teachers College Record, 111*(1), 124–63.

Phillips, N., Lawrence, T. B., & Hardy, C. (2000). Inter-organizational collaboration and the dynamics of institutional fields. *Journal of Management Studies, 37*(1).

Roderick, M., Nagaoka, J., Coca, V., & Moeller, E. (2008). *From high school to the future: Potholes on the road to college.* Research report. Chicago, IL: Consortium on Chicago School Research.

Schultz, J. L., & Mueller, D. (2006). *Effectiveness of programs to improve postsecondary education enrollment and success of underrepresented youth.* St. Paul, MN: Wilder Research.

Scott, J. (2000). *Social network analysis: A handbook*, 2nd ed. London, UK: Sage.

Simon, H. A. (1991). Bounded rationality and organizational learning. *Organization Science, 2*(1), 125–34.

Spillane, J. P., Hopkins, M., & Sweet, T. (2015). Intra- and inter-school interactions about instruction: Exploring the conditions for social capital development. *American Journal of Education, 122*(1), 71–110.

Standing, K., Judkins, D., Keller, B., & Shimshak, A. (2008). *Early outcomes of the GEAR UP program.* Final report. Washington, DC: US Department of Education.

Swail, W. S., & Perna, L. W. (2000). A view of the landscape. In *2001 Outreach program handbook*, 17–36. New York, NY: College Board.

Swail, W.S., & Perna, L.W. (2002). Pre-college outreach programs. In *Increasing access to college: Extending possibilities for all students*, edited by W. G. Tierney & L. S. Hagedorn, 15–34. Albany, NY: State University of New York Press.

Trist, E. (1983). Referent organizations and the development of inter-organizational domains. *Human Relations, 36*(3), 269–84.

Tsai, W. (2001). Knowledge transfer in intraorganizational networks: Effects of network position and absorptive capacity on business unit innovation and performance. *Academy of Management Journal, 44*(5), 996–1004.

Wasserman, S., & Faust, K. (1994). *Social network analysis: Methods and applications.* Cambridge, UK: Cambridge University Press.

Waters, M. (1994). *Modern sociological theory.* London, UK: Sage.

Chapter 6

Why Study with Friends?

A Relational Analysis of Students' Strategies to Integrate Social and Academic Life

JANICE MCCABE

> I definitely don't do my best work [with friends]. But I do busy work with them. If I have something serious, I'll go to the library. But anything quick and easy, I'll do in front of friends.
>
> —Amber,[1] UNH student

As the epigraph suggests, many college students acknowledge that studying with friends or relying on them for other help with their classes may not be the most productive use of their time. Some scholarly evidence backs this up (Arum & Roksa 2011). Yet I also find that nearly all college students study with friends at least occasionally. Why do students do it?

A relational approach points to new answers to this question. Academic life, particularly for residential college students, is embedded in social life. Moreover, most students strive to be successful both academically and socially (McCabe 2016; Moffatt 1989). I argue that students rarely achieve these goals separately; academic and social life are intertwined in numerous ways. By foregrounding relationships between people and the meanings of these relationships in particular networks and fields, a relational approach points to other useful outcomes of studying with friends besides academic ones, such as GPA or critical thinking scores. This chapter delves into this question using social network data and interviews with ninety-five students at three college campuses. By focusing on different types of institutions, I attempt to better account for cultural meanings and processes across the field of higher education and those that are tied to specific campuses. Pierre Bourdieu's concept of "field" is central to the relational approach I take here (Bourdieu & Wacquant 1992). Social networks do not have the same meaning across settings; instead, the social context of field gives value to particular social network structures (Winkle-Wagner & McCoy 2016).

In my previous work, I identify four strategies that students use to integrate social and academic life: engaging in instrumental help, emotional support, intellectual engagement, and competition with friends around academics (McCabe 2016). In this chapter, I explicitly use a relational approach. I argue that a relational lens sheds light on how and why students engage academically with friends using these strategies, even when it may seem more academically beneficial to keep friends separate from schoolwork. For example, rather than studying with friends, which students note is slower and less productive, they could study by themselves or with peers from class. Rather than asking a friend to quiz them before an exam, students could get a free tutor[2] or talk with the professor or teaching assistant. However, students also are doing relational work through studying together. They build and maintain their friendships, they refine their identity, and they are better able to balance academic and social life. At times, it makes them happier. Put simply, students study with friends to build and maintain these relationships and to succeed academically and socially. A relational approach also necessitates that students' strategies be contextualized within their friendship network structure and field—in this case, the field of higher education. I highlight how the relational benefits of friendship are tied to a student's network structure and the institution they attend.

Past Research on College Students, Friendship Networks, and Academics

Education scholars have long acknowledged the importance of peers for students' academic achievement. Some research views peers as negatively affecting or irrelevant to students' academic success (e.g., Armstrong & Hamilton 2013; Arum & Roksa 2011; Coleman 1961; Holland & Eisenhart

1990). One book, aptly titled *Academically Adrift*, documents a negative effect of studying with peers for undergraduates' learning (Arum & Roksa 2011). Based on the positive association between College Learning Assessment (CLA) performance—which measures critical thinking, analytical reasoning, problem solving, and writing—and time spent studying alone compared with the negative association with CLA performance and time spent studying with peers, Arum and Roksa argue that students would do better to study alone than with peers. This research, however, focusing narrowly on cognitive outcomes, does not differentiate between friends and other peers, and overlooks what peers are doing when they study together (Arum & Roksa 2011).

Other research, however, finds that peers and friends can be positive influences on students' success in college. For example, educational researchers stress peers' value through social involvement, integration, or engagement (Astin 1993; Kuh et al. 2005; Pascarella & Terenzini 2005; Tinto 1993, 2012) and sense of belonging (Hurtado & Carter 1997). In their review of three decades of research, Pascarella and Terenzini (2005, 187) refer to the effect of students' peers on cognitive and intellectual development in college as "modest but relatively consistent." They conclude, "Indeed, some studies suggest that one's peers may be an influence that is equal to, and in some cases perhaps even greater than, one's formal classroom experience" (Pascarella & Terenzini 2005, 187–88). Friends, as a specific group of peers, can also be academically valuable by talking about workloads and deadlines (Brooks 2007), trying out ideas with each other (Martinez Alemán 1997, 2000), having intellectual conversations about social issues (antonio 2001; Martinez Alemán 2000), and offering self-confidence and motivation (antonio 2004; Chambliss & Takacs 2014; Finn 2015).

In their review of the sociology of higher education, Stevens, Armstrong, and Arum (2008, 134) call for more network research, identifying "rich possibilities for scholars to map precisely the dynamics of undergraduate social networks." Few have taken up this call, despite frequent assertions of peers' importance for students' educational experiences. My prior work, based on research at a large public Midwestern university, shows how friendship networks both help and hinder academic and social success during and after college (McCabe 2016). By identifying three network types—tight-knitters, samplers, and compartmentalizers (e.g., those with a tight, cohesive friendship group, or those who move effortlessly between different social circles)—I demonstrate how racial, gender, and class disadvantages lead students to form different types of networks for support. By identifying network structures in this prior work (McCabe 2016), I took a social network approach, but not explicitly a relational one.

Social network analysis involves mapping connections to measure network structure. Sociologists have found many ways that network structure matters for individuals, arguing, for example, that "weak ties" lead to more productive job searches (Granovetter 1973). Networks can also constrain people (e.g., Portes 1998). Much network research on students' friendships assesses their composition, especially racial homogeneity, in high school (Kao & Joyner 2004; Moody 2001) and college (antonio 2004; McCabe 2016; Stearns, Buchmann, & Bonneau 2009). A second strand—referred to as "peer effects"—involves precisely measuring the effects of peers, such as roommates and dormmates, on students' academic outcomes (see review in Sacerdote 2011). Based on a longitudinal study at a college in India, Hasan and Bagde (2013) find that exam scores of students' randomly assigned roommates prior to college significantly effect students' own scores during their second semester of college. They find that scores of their friends and chosen study partners also correlate with students' scores; however, friends' and study partners' effects "declined in magnitude or disappeared" when controlling for students' and roommates' scores (Hasan & Bagde 2013). Economists and other peer effects researchers have focused on quantifying how much peers matter and grappling with measurement and modeling issues, particularly that friendships are not randomly formed. Erikson (2013) refers to this type of social network research as "formalism" because of its focus on social forms or structure.

Relational sociology, on the other hand, centers relationships and interactions (Emirbayer 1997; Erikson 2013; Finn 2015). Whereas "social network analysis takes as its fundamental unit of analysis the relationships between actors," relational theory "has a more specific meaning that encompasses strong claims about the primacy of experience, which are not embraced by many researchers in social networks" (Erikson 2013, 221–22). In other words, a relational approach aligns with social network research, but social network research is not necessarily based in relational theory. A relational approach highlights agency and social structure and their duality (Emirbayer 1997; Erikson 2013). In this project, I take a relational approach to social network theory by tying students' experiences in college—within the field of higher education because this setting gives value to particular networks—with the structure of their networks. I examine both the structure and meaning of students' friendship networks, pairing quantitative measures and mapping of network structure (including the figures discussed later in this chapter) with qualitative measures of students' experiences and meanings across three postsecondary institutions. My focus on friendship structure and experience provides a unique relational window into strategies undergraduates use to involve friends academically and separate them from academic life.

Methods

In this chapter, I draw on data from a comparative case study of students' friendships at three types of postsecondary institutions—a small elite private college (Dartmouth College), a large public university (University of New Hampshire, UNH), and a nonresidential community college (Manchester Community College, MCC). Choosing institutions in similar locations that differ in size, selectivity, residential life, and campus culture allows me to leverage strengths of case study design. In the broader project, I emphasize the historical, institutional, and demographic contexts (Yin 2014) of these three institutions.

In line with a case study approach, my focus is on identifying patterns within and across institutions, rather than being generalizable to specific populations (Small 2009). I recruited participants through a range of clubs and organizations (e.g., identity-based clubs for racial groups and first-generation college students, academic clubs, and Greek organizations) and by posting flyers on and near each campus. To supplement these recruitment efforts, I asked participants for suggestions of people to speak with, noting that I was particularly interested in people who may have different experiences or opinions than the participant.

In 2015–17, I interviewed ninety-five students: thirty-five from Dartmouth, thirty-four from UNH, and twenty-six from MCC. At Dartmouth and UNH, most students I interviewed were finishing up their second year or starting their third; at MCC, most interviews were with students in at least their second year of college. During the interviews, I systematically collected a list of each participant's friends and their perception of whether each friend knew each other friend; because it is from the perspective of the participant, this is referred to as "egocentric" network data. Rather than limiting the friends students could name—for example, to those attending their same college—I followed their social networks where they were meaningful for participants, even when they crossed campus boundaries. I attended to power dynamics in and across networks (Bourdieu &

Wacquant 1992) by understanding not just the structure of the networks but how students experience them. The in-depth interviews enabled this approach. I will interview participants every two to five years to assess how institutional factors and friendship networks affect their long-term success; follow-up interviews began in 2018.

In constructing each case, I draw on multiple sources of evidence (Yin 2014), specifically fieldnotes from my observations in public spaces (libraries, cafeterias, etc.), archival documents written by and about the institutions (in local papers, *The Princeton Review*, etc.), student surveys and interviews, and egocentric network data on students' friendships. This approach helps maximize validity through triangulation of data and the depth gained through interviewing as well as to maximize reliability by triangulation along with the semi-structured interview design and standardized collection of network data. Most of the data in this chapter come from the interviews; however, the other methodological approaches often helped me arrive at the understandings presented here.

I analyzed these data using Atlas.ti and Netdraw.[3] After entering my fieldnotes and transcribed interviews into Atlas.ti, I used the constant comparative method (Glaser & Strauss 1967) to pursue confirming patterns and negative cases. For example, I deductively coded for types of friends' academic involvement (e.g., intellectual, emotional, and instrumental), constantly returning to the data to compare across patterns and categories. Inductive coding involved the creation of new codes from the data—such as cases where they studied by themselves. Using Netdraw, I generated the friendship network maps (i.e., sociograms) discussed later in this chapter.

Results

Strategies Students Use to Integrate Friends and Academics

During the interviews, I invited students to tell me about their friends, including describing the last time they spent with friends, what things they typically do with friends, and who they talk to about school. Later in the interview, I asked more pointed questions about how often and with whom they engage in different aspects of academic life. Based on both types of discussions, I found four ways that college students at these campuses engage in academic life with their friends: (1) instrumental assistance, (2) emotional support and encouragement, (3) intellectual discussions, and (4) competition.[4] First, friends provide instrumental help with academics by, for example, studying together, studying alongside each other, proofreading papers, and waking each other up for class. Second, friends provide emotional support and engagement regarding academics by venting, motivating each other, and expressing concern about a friend's grades or assignments. Third, friends engage in intellectual discussions, such as talking about ideas from class or broader political, social, or cultural issues. Fourth, students engage in competition with friends by comparing grades, scores, and successes with internships or other opportunities in a sort of "friendly competition," as students often called it.

A Relational Lens on Students' Strategies

I started coding by classifying whether each respondent used these strategies as well as the subtypes within it. For example, for "instrumental assistance," I coded whether the respondent studied with friends. For some students, this was easy to categorize: they studied regularly with friends or they did not study with friends. For the majority of respondents, however, it seemed like categorizing studying with friends as a dichotomy or even trying to track how many hours a week they spent doing so failed to capture the complexities of this process. A majority of students described times they studied with friends and times they did not—and, importantly, would not want to.

A relational approach helped explain this process. Specifically, it helped identify patterns in how students' strategies operate in the field of higher education as well as differences within it (i.e., by friendship network structure and campus). A relational approach thus acknowledges this duality: students' agency and the limits of the structures they create (Erikson 2013; Emirbayer 1997). Students' descriptions of the time they spend with friends reveal that they often seek to separate academic and social life, yet they find these two spheres difficult to keep separate, particularly in a residential college context. Echoing the findings of past research (McCabe 2016; Moffatt 1989), nearly every student I spoke with had social and academic goals for their college experience: for example, they hoped to have fun and graduate, or they hoped to make friends and do well in their classes.

Students also faced competing demands for achieving these goals, and the demands differed slightly by campus. For the community college students, it was often demands between their jobs and classes, sometimes adding family demands or friends to the mix. For the four-year college students, the demands were often between their extracurricular activities, friends, and classes, sometimes adding varsity sports or jobs. Regardless of the specific demands, all students faced constraints on the number of available hours to meet their goals. Thus, there are ways that students' experiences are similar across the field of higher education and ways that they are campus-specific.

Some students sought to meet both goals by separating friends from academics. However, the nature of four-year residential colleges makes academic and social life nearly impossible to separate (McCabe 2016). Although students talked about dividing their days or weeks into academic or social (for example, daytime is academics, nighttime is social; or midterm and finals weeks are more academic and other points in the term are more social), they were rarely able to achieve a clean divide. Even though community college students were more easily able to separate academic and social life, they felt pressures because they typically had greater demands on their time from paid work and family responsibilities.

Therefore, encouraging students to study by themselves or, more generally, dismissing the time they spend with friends as getting in the way of academic achievement is not wise. It ignores the interconnectedness of academic and social life and the relational benefits of mixing them. In the following section, I explore what a relational approach reveals about students' strategies for integrating academic and social life by focusing on students' experiences with one of the four types of strategies: studying with friends.

Relational Benefits of Studying with Friends

The quote that opens this chapter suggests that students may realize that studying with friends is not the most productive way to study, yet they do it. Here, I use a relational lens to more closely examine their explanations and how such explanations differ across friendship network structures.

Students' descriptions of studying with friends reveal that they seek to meet both social and academic goals through this activity. Put simply, they study with friends because it is fun. Students noted that it can feel "lonely," "sad," "depressing," or "dark" to spend hours by yourself reading or studying. Jorge told me that during his first year at Dartmouth, he hunkered down during finals period to study by himself:

> And I realized I was missing people. I was just like, wow, today was a really depressing day. I didn't see the sun because it was all overcast. I didn't talk to anyone or, like, really interact with anyone, other than [saying] "hi" [as I was] walking down the street to get food. And that was kind of depressing. . . . I don't want to do this again. I should definitely keep people in my life [and] at least once a day talk to them. I definitely found myself brought down and sad.

Students at all three campuses described times they regretted spending so much time studying by themselves, even when they felt it was necessary to perform well academically. I was surprised by how frequently students told me that even though this strategy led them to the grades they were hoping for, they did not intend to do it again. This was the case for Jorge. Timothy, a UNH student, told me how he did not want to share the "regrets" of his older brother, who graduated from UNH in three years (rather than four) to save on tuition costs, and consequently felt that he lost out on having "fun—that was one thing he regretted." Timothy took his brother's advice, making sure to enjoy college and spend time with friends, including studying together. He admitted, "sometimes our study sessions would turn into, like, just playing video games. It wasn't efficient, but [it was] pretty fun." Even students who mostly studied alone, such as Kate, a Dartmouth student, saw the emotional benefits of occasionally studying with friends: "I would get burned out if I just kept to my academics like all the time." When I asked her about the last time she studied with a friend, Kate described grabbing a quick dinner together and studying separate subjects together in the library: "we laugh a lot" and "we have fun just hanging out." Most often, students balanced casual (and less productive) studying with friends with more serious studying alone. Though less common, some students on each campus balanced casual studying with friends with more serious studying with classmates (not considered "friends"). Students told me that it can be lonely to study by yourself and less lonely to do so with friends.

In addition to being "fun," studying with friends can also matter for a student's sense of self, including feelings of belonging or considering oneself a "dedicated student." For example, Lisa, a Black student who was the first in her family to attend college, described her friendship group as important for helping her realize that she belonged at UNH and could succeed here.

She described how she kept the same group of friends, whom she met in class: "They were really important for me, like getting through the first two years. Um, [*laughs*] really important because we all studied together." Studying together became a regular part of their friendship, which helped Lisa see herself as a college student and a legitimate member of the UNH community. Such findings build on other research showing that talking about friends can be "identity work" that helps solidify students' sense of self (e.g., Anthony & McCabe 2015). Studying with friends reinforced the importance of students' academic identities.

Studying with friends also helped strengthen students' relationships with those friends. Time shared together matters: rather than only having exclusively "social time" to spend with friends, students are able to spend more time with friends by studying together. This worked to strengthen one-on-one friendships (e.g., for Mira and her friend Ciara in figure 6.1) and also to strengthen groups (e.g., for Heidi in figure 6.2). In the sociograms, the largest dot is the student I interviewed, the other dots are their friends, and the lines between friends indicate if the participant believed their friends knew each other. In figure 6.1, Mira, a community college student, has one friend she studies with (Ciara, who is also an MCC student), and she finds that the relationship grows stronger as they spend time together studying. With full-time work, Mira has little time for studying or hanging out with friends. Studying with Ciara does not always help her improve her GPA because they often both struggle to understand the material, but it does strengthen their friendship and help them feel like they belong at MCC. Kira, a Dartmouth student who does not have a paid job, explained the trade-off she experienced in time spent studying with friends:

> Usually [studying is] it's by myself, but if my friends are like, "Do you want to go study?" I'll go. But I'm [thinking] like, all right, I'm not going to get as much done as I could. Do you know what I mean? So, it's kind of a sacrifice. And usually I just prefer to go [study] by myself.

When I asked, "Why would you choose to study with them, then, if it's a sacrifice?" Kira replied:

> I guess it would be that social element. Like, all right, I'll go hang out with my friends because, like, they're my friends.

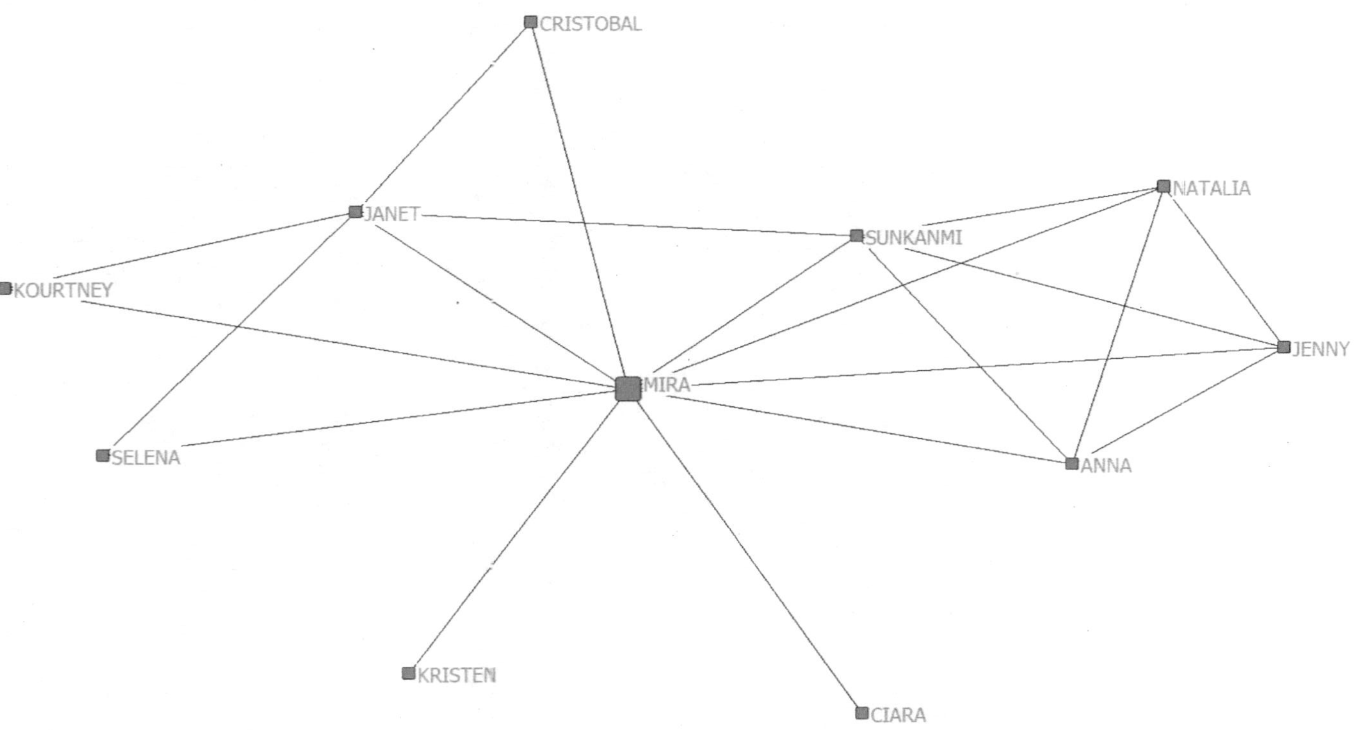

Figure 6.1. Mira's friendship network. *Source:* Janice McCabe.

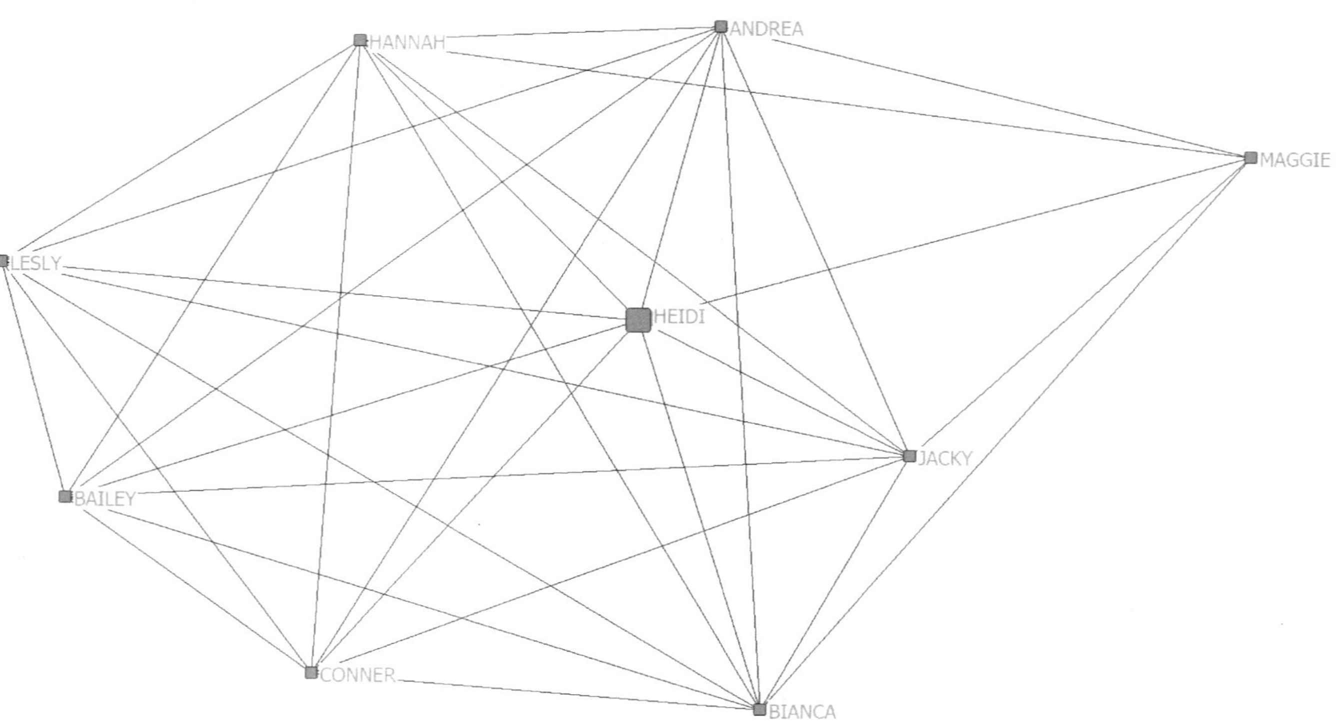

Figure 6.2. Heidi's friendship network. *Source:* Janice McCabe.

> But it's kinda like, this isn't probably what's best for me right now. But at the same time, it's, you know, hanging out with someone who just gets you.

For Kira, choosing to study with friends is a sacrifice because of the amount of school work she has compared with the available hours in her schedule; however, she finds times that the benefits to her sense of self and relationships outweigh those effects on her GPA. Students study with friends because of these relational benefits.

Heidi's tight-knit friendship network is shown in figure 6.2, and she believes that studying together is something that "of course" her college friends do together. Unlike Kira, who describes herself as "academically focused" and "serious," Heidi is a recreation management major at UNH who describes her workload as "easy" and "no big deal." Before our interview, Heidi had been "hanging out doing homework" in her living room with her three roommates. When I asked if this was typical, she replied,

> Yeah. We're always in the living room. It's kind of weird if people are in their room [bedroom] doing their homework. . . . My room's big, there's a desk and everything. But it's just, in our apartment, it's a known thing, everyone goes to the [dining room] table and does their work or sits on the couch. . . . Because everyone just wants to be hanging out doing work. We're kind of always hanging out. Like no one's really ever just in their room, unless you're like napping or something.

It is doubtful that Heidi's most productive work location is in the living room, but spending that time studying with friends reinforces their bonds and their academic identities. Rather than studying at her desk in her large bedroom, she prefers to study with her friends. Studying with friends strengthens these relationships regardless of whether students consider themselves academically focused (like Kira) or mostly unengaged (like Heidi).

Studying with friends can also bring about other academic benefits. The most common benefits students cited were motivational and emotional support gained by studying together. They also discussed instrumental benefits, such as tips about classes to take or someone to proofread an essay before they turn it in. For example, Sophia, a UNH student, explained, "I'm surrounded by some pretty intelligent friends who I feel help me sometimes be academically serious as well." When I asked how her friends help her in this way, she explains that they go to the library together to get books as well as "just honestly the encouragement about going abroad [a program she will participate in next year] and just doing what's best for me and just them being my back up and saying, 'yeah, that's really good for you' [or] 'that's a really awesome job.'" Sophia did not talk to her friends much about academics; instead, she saw her friends as more important for her social life as a member of a high-status sorority on campus. Therefore, the emotional benefits she gained from these limited times that her friends did connect academically were all the more significant for her. Another UNH student, Timothy, described a different style of encouragement to study that he felt from studying with friends. Timothy's network is shown in figure 6.3. Unlike Sophia, Timothy's encouragement was not something that friends directly said to him; he felt it just from being in the same space as other people who were also devoted to schoolwork. He explained: "I study sometimes with friends who I don't share any classes with, like people in my dorm, people from my backpacking trip, we just sit in the lounge and do homework, and probably talk more than do homework." I asked if it was helpful to study in this way, to which he replied, "Um, I guess so. I probably don't get as much done as studying on my own, but it's also nicer [and] it's easier to say, 'I'll study tonight in the lounge with friends' rather than in my room all alone or at the library. It's more encouraging." Studying with friends can facilitate emotional and instrumental support along with reinforcing a strong academic identity.

Where the friend is located within the network also influences students' strategies. For example, the friends Timothy studied with most often were in the largest tight-knit group in his network: the right-hand side of figure 6.3. With his "study friends" connected to each other, he found it easier to fall into studying together without constantly needing to make plans to do so. This was also true of Heidi's more casual studying with friends, which did not require planning. In contrast, Mira's study friend is disconnected from anyone else in her network: Ciara in the bottom right of figure 6.2. Studying in one-on-one friendships—such as the one between Mira and Ciara—can be "fun" and strengthen their academic identities and relationships. Yet the process through which this network structure leads to these benefits is more fragile. By this I mean that it depends on both partners to continue the relationship. It takes planning. Mira and Ciara have been able to continue to study together by scheduling

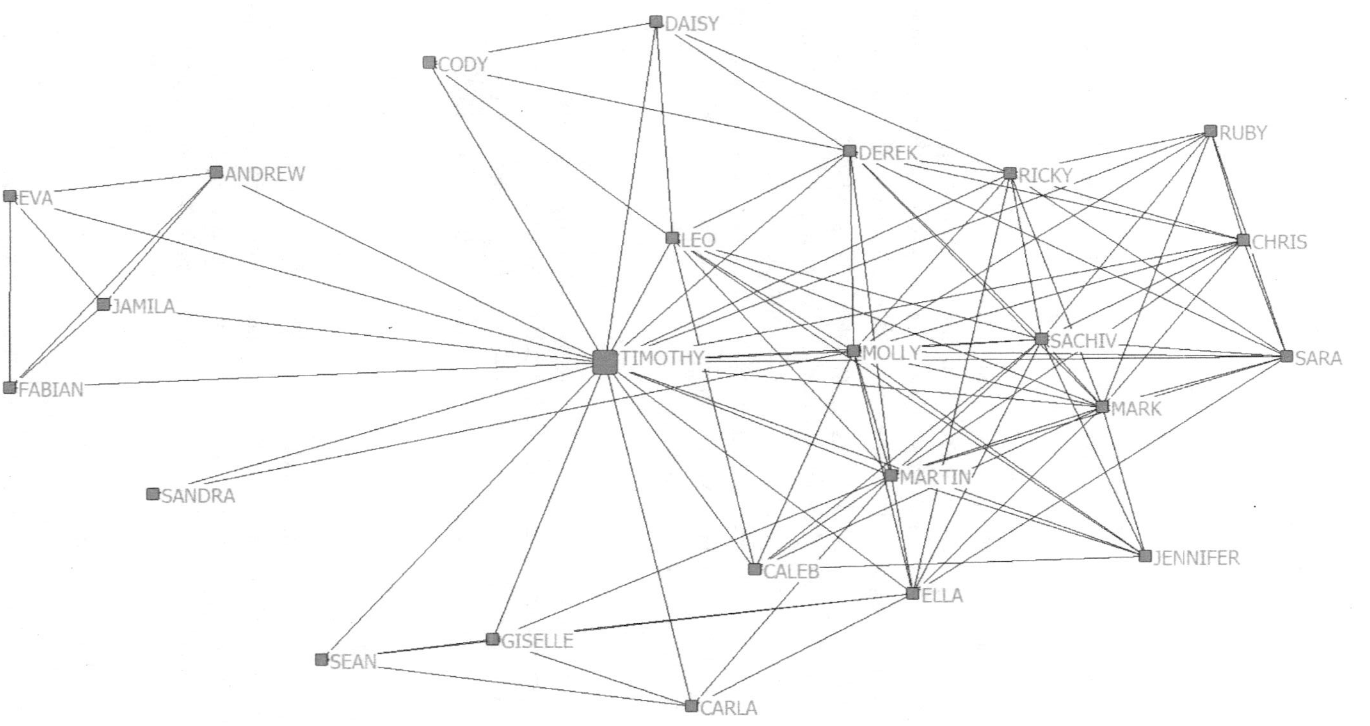

Figure 6.3. Timothy's friendship network. *Source:* Janice McCabe.

classes together, so they will be physically present at MCC at the same time. I suspect that this will get harder as they need to fulfill their final graduation requirements.

I find that students' strategies to integrate social and academic life operate differently in the three campuses that I studied. That is, students engaged in the same strategies, but they had varying meanings at the different campuses and the process unfolded differently.

At Dartmouth, students typically had many choices for studying with friends—"too many" choices, according to some of my participants. Most had enough options that they could always study with friends and study with a variety of friends. This meant that to carve out time to study by themselves, they had to turn down invitations. To maintain these relationships, they also had to say "yes" (i.e., study with friends) often enough. Whereas Dartmouth students did not struggle to find others studying during the week, staying in to study on a weekend night could be something that brought friends together. For example, Sasha explained how "it's nice to have people that I can be studying with and who aren't gonna be like, 'Why are you sitting inside on a Saturday night?' " At times, friends also help students achieve balance, so they aren't "too social" or "too academic" as Sophia explained:

> We [friends] all help each other, so it'll be something like, for friends that have a test in two weeks and [say], "I'm gonna stay in and make a study sheet," and it's like, "Do you need to do that tonight, or can you just relax a little bit?" or, you know, "Hey, you have a paper due soon. You should really do this outline now instead of pushing it off for tomorrow." So, we just keep each other on track and make sure we're, like, maintaining that healthy balance.

Students at all three campuses described times when friends encouraged them to study or devote more time to academics, but Dartmouth students in particular appreciated specific friends who helped them avoid becoming "overly focused" on academics. As Sophia put it, friends "keep each other on track" by putting academic and social workloads and pacing in perspective.

UNH students more often had a core group of friends with whom they study. This pattern is shown in figures 6.2 and 6.3, despite many other differences in Heidi's and Timothy's friendship networks and their respective self-descriptions as academically unengaged and serious. Timothy saw his devotion to his studies as something that set him apart from most other UNH students, whom he saw as more socially oriented. Heidi regularly studied with a group of friends (the tight-knit group shown in figure 6.2), but they typically studied different material alongside each other. Other students, like Timothy, studied with a group of friends (those on the lower right side of figure 6.3) who were familiar with the same material and could answer questions or offer other instrumental help. At most, UNH students studied with two groups—general studying alongside friends (often roommates) and those in their subject area (who may or may not be "friends"). More typical was having one friendship group with whom they studied.

At MCC, students typically had one (or at most a couple of) friends whom they studied with. This meant that the community college students did not have the flexibility or the demands on them to study with friends as in the other two institutions. Some MCC students never studied with friends, but most recognized that they could combine their academic and social goals (e.g., make friends and graduate) by at least occasionally studying with a friend or two. Even the MCC students who studied most frequently with friends had only one group they studied with; none of my MCC participants had multiple groups with whom they studied. At MCC, students did not live together on campus, and most did not live with another student or friend, so studying together took planning to meet up in the library, lounge, or off-campus location (i.e., apartment or coffee shop). Relative to the two residential campuses, it was unusual for MCC students to talk about studying with friends as helping strengthen their friendships. Two MCC students talked about completing schoolwork while hanging out with groups of friends who were not students; their friends would watch TV or play video games and they would study. This allowed each to spend time with their friendship group and do homework; thereby strengthening both their relationships and student identity. At Dartmouth, most students expected that friends would study together, whereas this norm was generally true only among selected friends at UNH and is not a norm at MCC. In sum, I found structural constraints and differing norms across these campuses; thus, studying with friends was a strategy that played out differently across institutions.

Conclusion

A relational approach brings not just new but more complete answers to the question of how friends matter for college students' success. Existing research tends to focus squarely on the academic consequences of studying with peers (Arum & Roksa 2011; Sacerdote 2011) or the identity effects of talking about friendship (Anthony & McCabe 2015) or descriptively noting the composition of students' friendship networks (e.g., antonio 2011; Moody 2001; Stearns, Buchmann, & Bonneau 2009). Their focus tends to be on social forms or structure. A relational approach centers relationships and meaning; thus, rather than assuming that a particular friendship structure works a certain way, a relational approach sheds light on the meaning of a particular social network structure for its members as well as how it operates in a particular field. In this way, a relational approach to students' friendship networks acknowledges students' agency in creating and maintain these ties and the constraints of the field. A relational approach acknowledges that fields are not static but are shaped by the actions of participants. A strictly formalist approach to network analysis (Erikson 2013), for example, might stop at identifying that different network structures exist or are predominant at different institutions without also acknowledging the meaning of these networks and how these meanings shape how students balance academic and social life.

In contrast to claims from research, parents, and students themselves that time "studying with peers . . . was not time well spent, at least not for developing general collegiate skills" (Arum & Roksa 2014, 34), I find that the time can be well spent if the goal is balancing academic and social life, developing a student identity, or maintaining friendships. Students are doing relational work by engaging in academic activities with friends. The effects may not be direct ones on their GPA or other academic outcomes, but they may indirectly affect academics through motivation and other emotional benefits. Engaging in academics with friends, such as studying together, can strengthen a student's academic identities and friendships. It can also make them happier and keep them in college.

The differences I found in how "study friends" are positioned in students' friendship networks have implications for research and practice. Future survey research should go beyond asking students to report how much time they spend studying with peers to include details about the person and activity. Although the level of detail I gathered from interviews is not easily achieved in a survey format, it would be especially useful to know whether they studied with a group or with an individual and if they were friends or just peers. Survey researchers could ask about frequency of discussion with specific friends about specific topics, including course material and assignments, grades, future jobs, postbaccalaureate educational plans, financial concerns, and personal or family issues. Although not exhaustive of discussions students might have with friends, these topics capture the level of engagement with day-to-day academic life between friends and tap instrumental and emotional aspects of friendships likely to support college success (McCabe 2016). Students and those supporting them (e.g., faculty, administrators, and parents) may also benefit from reflecting on whether students have "study friends" or a single "study friend" and how connected these friends are within their network. If study friends are disconnected from others in the network, students likely need to put more energy into maintaining these ties and their academic focus than if they were tightly connected. This challenge appears even greater on a campus with weak norms of studying with friends. Like Mira's experience at the community college, it may take extensive planning to schedule classes with friends to be physically present on campus at the same time. On other campuses, where the norm is to study with friends, students would be wise to reflect on when they would benefit from studying by themselves and invest in friends who "keep each other on track," including helping each other avoid becoming "overly focused" on academics. Although students are often doing relational work while studying with friends, studying with friends is not always the best strategy.

While there are certainly reasons in addition to relational ones, like personality and academic skills and commitment, that affect when and how students engage academically with friends, recognizing the relational ones is important for gaining a fuller understanding of students' actions and beliefs. Future research should explore other patterns and power dynamics, particularly how race, ethnicity, class, gender, and major at the individual, friendship network, and campus affect the relational benefits students gain from studying together. For example, Lisa's experience with her same-race study friends suggests that studying with friends might be more effective on sense of belonging for those from underrepresented groups. Major may matter, too, specifically the ease or extent to which students get to know others in their classes through small group discussions and collaborative assignments. The relational approach I take considers agency and social structure and their duality. It reveals much about the interconnectedness of academic and social life across the field of higher education. A relational approach also shows how friends can matter on the path to academic and social success.

Notes

1. I use pseudonyms for all participants and their friends.

2. All three campuses had some free tutoring available; Dartmouth had more options than the other campuses.

3. For the broader project, I also used Gephi to generate friendship network maps and quantitative measures—such as betweenness centrality, modularity, and density—and I used Stata to generate descriptive statistics to compare across institutions.

4. For more discussion of these four types and where aspects of each appear in previous literature (e.g., Brooks 2007; Martinez Aléman 1997), see McCabe (2016).

References

Anthony, A. K., & McCabe, J. (2015). Friendship talk as identity work: Defining the self through friend relationships. *Symbolic Interaction*, *38*(1), 64–82.

antonio, a. l. (2001). Diversity and the influence of friendship groups in college. *Review of Higher Education*, *25*(1), 63–89.

antonio, a. l. (2004). The influence of friendship groups on intellectual self-confidence and educational aspirations in college. *Journal of Higher Education*, *75*(4), 446–71.

Armstrong, E. A., & Hamilton, L. T. (2013). *Paying for the party: How college maintains inequality*. Cambridge, MA: Harvard University Press.

Arum, R., & Roksa, J. (2011). *Academically adrift: Limited learning on college campuses*. Chicago, IL: University of Chicago Press.

Arum, R., & Roksa, J. (2014). *Aspiring adults adrift: Tentative transitions of college graduates*. Chicago, IL: University of Chicago Press.

Astin, A. W. (1993). *What matters in college? Four critical years revisited*. San Francisco, CA: Jossey-Bass.

Bourdieu, P., & Wacquant, L. J. (1992). *An invitation to reflexive sociology*. Chicago, IL: University of Chicago Press.

Brooks, R. (2007). Friends, peers, and higher education. *British Journal of Sociology of Education*, *28*(6), 693–707.

Chambliss, D. F., & Takacs, C. G. (2014). *How college works*. Cambridge, MA: Harvard University Press.

Coleman, J. (1961). *The adolescent society: The social life of the teenager and its impact on education*. New York, NY: Free Press.

Emirbayer, M. (1997). Manifesto for a relational sociology. *American Journal of Sociology*, *103*(2), 281–317.

Erikson, E. (2013). Formalist and relationalist theory in social network analysis. *Sociological Theory*, *31*(3), 219–42.

Finn, K. (2015). *Personal life, young women and higher education: A relational approach to student and graduate experiences*. New York, NY: Palgrave Macmillan.

Glaser, B. G., & Strauss, A. L. (1967). *The discovery of grounded theory: Strategies for qualitative research*. Chicago, IL: Aldine.

Granovetter, M. S. (1973). The strength of weak ties. *American Journal of Sociology*, *78*(6), 1360–80.

Hasan, S., & Bagde, S. (2013). The mechanics of social capital and academic performance in an Indian college. *American Sociological Review*, *78*(6), 1009–32.

Holland, D. C., & Eisenhart, M. E. (1990). *Educated in romance: Women, achievement, and college culture*. Chicago, IL: University of Chicago Press.

Hurtado, S., & Carter, D. F. (1997). Effects of college transition and perceptions of the campus racial climate on Latino students' sense of belonging. *Sociology of Education*, *70*(4), 324–45.

Kao, G., & Joyner, K. (2004). Do race and ethnicity matter among friends? Activities among interracial, interethnic, and intraethnic adolescent friends. *Sociological Quarterly*, *45*(3), 557–73.

Kuh, G. D., Kinzie, J., Schuh, J. H., Whitt, E. J., & Associates. (2005). *Student success in college: Creating conditions that matter*. San Francisco, CA: Jossey-Bass.

Martinez Alemán, A. M. (1997). Understanding and investigating female friendship's educative value. *Journal of Higher Education*, *68*, 119–59.

Martinez Alemán, A. M. (2000). Race talks: Undergraduate women of color and female friendships. *Review of Higher Education*, *23*, 133–52.

McCabe, J. (2016). *Connected in college: How friendship networks matter for academic and social success*. Chicago, IL: University of Chicago Press.

Moffatt, M. (1989). *Coming of age in New Jersey: College and American culture*. New Brunswick, NJ: Rutgers University Press.

Moody, J. (2001). Race, school integration and friendship segregation in America. *American Journal of Sociology*, *107*(3), 679–716.

Pascarella, E. T., & Terenzini, P. T. (2005). *How college affects students: Volume 2: A Third Decade of Research*. San Francisco, CA: Jossey-Bass.

Portes, A. (1998). Social capital: Its origins and applications in modern sociology. *Annual Review of Sociology*, *24*, 1–24.

Sacerdote, B. (2011). Peer effects in education: How might they work, how big are they and how much do we know thus far? In *Handbook of the economics of education: Volume 3*, edited by E. A. Hanushek, S. Machin, & L. Woessmann, 249–77. Waltham, MA: Elsevier.

Small, M. (2009). "How many cases do I need?" On science and the logic of case selection in field-based research. *Ethnography*, *10*, 5–38.

Stearns, E., Buchmann, C., & Bonneau, K. (2009). Interracial friendships in the transition to college: Do birds of a feather flock together once they leave the nest? *Sociology of Education*, *82*, 173–95.

Stevens, M. L., Armstrong, E. A., & Arum, R. (2008). Sieve, incubator, temple, hub: Empirical and theoretical advances in the sociology of higher education. *Annual Review of Sociology*, *34*, 127–51.

Tinto, V. (1993). *Leaving college: Rethinking the causes and cures of student attrition* (2nd ed.). Chicago, IL: University of Chicago Press.

Tinto, V. (2012). *Completing college: Rethinking institutional action*. Chicago, IL: University of Chicago Press.

Winkle-Wagner, R., & McCoy, D. L. (2016). Entering the (postgraduate) field: Underrepresented students' acquisition of cultural and social capital in graduate school preparation programs. *Journal of Higher Education*, *87*(2), 178–205.

Yin, R. K. (2014). *Case study research: Design and methods* (5th ed.). Thousand Oaks, CA: Sage.

Chapter 7

What Can Relational Sociology Reveal about College Writing and Remediation?

MICHAEL LANFORD

Background: The Problem of Remediation in US Higher Education

To meet the labor market demands of a twenty-first-century knowledge economy, the United States—like other economically developed nations—forecasts a need for more graduates with college degrees. By most estimates, 60 percent of the US citizenry will need a postsecondary credential to be competitive for future jobs (e.g., Lumina Foundation 2014). Nevertheless, as of 2016, only 34.2 percent of Americans twenty-five years of age and older held a four-year college credential (US Census Bureau 2017). As a result, the retention and graduation rates of undergraduate students have received amplified scrutiny from policy makers and influential nonprofit organizations focused on improving degree completion outcomes in US colleges and universities. The first year of college, in particular, has been identified as a principal exit point for many undergraduates. According to fall 2015 statistics from the National Student Clearinghouse Research Center (2017), 26.6 percent of all full-time and part-time students left college after their initial year.

Students who need remediation in English language writing, English language reading, or mathematics face even greater challenges.[1] Between

40 percent and 60 percent of US college students need remediation in one or more subjects during their first year of enrollment (Jimenez, Sargrad, Morales, & Thompson 2016). Yet students who enroll in remedial coursework are less likely to complete their intended credentials than their peers (Clotfelter, Ladd, Muschkin, & Vigdor 2015). Students in remedial coursework are also more likely to be older, hail from an urban high school, and fit the criteria of a "nontraditional" student in terms of previous employment and educational experiences (Attewell, Lavin, Domina, & Levey 2006). Estimates of the nationwide annual costs of remediation vary from $3 billion (Complete College America 2012) to $7 billion (Scott-Clayton, Crosta, & Belfield 2012). Therefore, critics of remedial coursework argue that it presents a major obstacle for students seeking a postsecondary credential and exacerbates inequities for underrepresented students in higher education while being prohibitively expensive. From a national policy perspective, then, research that contributes to a deeper understanding of remedial coursework is vital if the United States is to increase degree attainment and ameliorate disparities that threaten to undermine greater social equity and individual opportunity.

Since the beginning of the twenty-first century, a growing number of studies have cast doubt about the efficiency of remedial education and its net positive influence on student outcomes. The Community College Research Center (CCRC) at Columbia University has been notably active in questioning the effectiveness of remedial programs, contending that previous research was far too dependent on single-site studies and nonrandom comparisons of different groups of students. Moreover, CCRC researchers asserted that what constitutes college readiness is unclear, assessments are inconsistently deployed between institutions, and educational reforms to the sector are necessary (e.g., Bailey, Jaggars, & Scott-Clayton 2013; Scott-Clayton, Crosta, & Belfield 2012).

Over the past several years, other researchers have refined the CCRC's initial critiques. Boatman and Long (2018), for instance, indicated that some students who enroll with lower levels of academic preparation may indeed benefit from remedial coursework. Other researchers have explored the effects of accelerated coursework (e.g., Jaggars, Hodara, Cho, & Xu 2015) and corequisite coursework (e.g., Belfield, Jenkins, & Lahr 2016) as a reform substitute for traditional remedial classes.

These studies have been helpful in highlighting serious issues associated with remediation. However, in what follows, I first argue that the recent forms of inquiry employed to understand remediation are limited in their methodological and theoretical purview. Afterward, I consider how the use of relational sociology can ameliorate some of these gaps in our understanding of remediation, specifically with regard to writing. The remainder of the chapter consist of a brief methodological description, presentation, and analysis of three narratives from ethnographic fieldwork that use a relational approach to studying remediation and college writing. These three narratives will depict how relational sociology can be effectively used to augment our knowledge about student experiences in remedial coursework and shed light on the relationships that are essential for student success.

Gaps in Understanding Remediation

Methodological Gaps

The majority of research on remedial education to date has produced an abundance of outcome-oriented quantitative data about students' college trajectories. Although extremely useful for determining *what* might work, these approaches have offered little in the way of understanding *how* or *why* a specific educational program or reform of remediation works. This methodologically derived gap in our understanding of remediation is consequential for two reasons. First, identifying a causal relationship between remediation and educational attainment remains elusive, since students are not randomly assigned to remedial education (Levin & Calcagno 2008). Second, a simple comparison of nonremedial students with remedial students is inherently problematic because precollege differences are likely to influence the final results (Boatman 2012). These factors complicate the substantial body of quantitative research that has been accumulated, particularly over the past ten years.

Second, the present focus on outcome-related data from math coursework has resulted in comparatively little analogous data about the specific challenges students face in the writing classroom. In the modern knowledge economy, critical thinking skills, the ability to communicate with different audiences, and the competencies associated with exposure to different cultures are progressively in high demand (Frey & Osborne 2017). Although many academic subjects contribute to the cultivation of creativity and social intelligence, writing is a unique skill that promotes dialectic thinking, deep understanding of a given topic, and an understanding of the relationship between communication, cultural expectations, and social values. For these reasons, I maintain that rigorous qualitative research on first-year writing is at least equally important to quantitative assessments of student math outcomes.

Theoretical Gaps

A theoretical issue has arisen from the concentrated attention on math outcomes—namely, that researchers have implicitly presumed that learning is solely a cognitive process. Hence, when explaining their findings, researchers have consistently speculated that contemporary reforms to remediation, such as acceleration, improve individual student motivation. According to this line of reasoning, a motivated student who is able to progress quickly through credit-bearing classes will cognitively develop academic skills more rapidly and demonstrate measurable improvement (Hodara & Xu 2016; Logue, Watanabe-Rose, & Douglas 2016).

For a study of first-year writing, however, theories involving cognition and student motivation may not adequately explain student development and success. As the past forty years of research on college composition have demonstrated, writing is not simply a cognitive process; it is also a sociocultural process, by the writer's initiation and continued exposure to identifiable discourse communities (Prior 2006; Vygotsky 1934/1986). From a sociocultural perspective, scholastic success depends on a student's immersion into a discourse community that, as described by Gee (2015), shares "ways of behaving, interacting, valuing, thinking, believing, speaking, and (often) reading and writing" (4) with the student's first-year writing coursework. For some students, exposure to academic conventions of grammar, rhetorical thinking, and/or paper organization might occur in the home, particularly if a parent is college-educated. For other students, a college-preparatory curriculum that emphasizes the essay genres and research expectations of higher education can suffice.

Unfortunately, countless students are not exposed to the conventions of college discourse that would enable them to succeed in first-year writing. In many high schools, students on a college prep track receive special attention and feedback on their writing from English teachers conversant with college expectations. Conversely, students in general English experience a curriculum specifically designed for success on high school standardized exams, where rudimentary elements of grammar, sentence structure, and punctuation assume importance over research, organization, and rhetorical skills that augur success in first-year college writing. As researchers have consistently shown, these educational tracks inscribe existing divides based on ethnicity, race, and economic class (Oakes & Guiton 1995; Callahan 2005). Thus, as I have argued elsewhere, students from low-income and first-generation backgrounds frequently enter the collegiate landscape as "outsiders" who rapidly need to make sense of the implicit academic expectations of their instructor (Lanford 2018).

In summary, we have surprisingly little firsthand knowledge about student perspectives on remedial coursework, the instructional practices that students find most helpful, the resources that are essential for student success, or the valuable relationships that introduce students to academic discourse communities. To use a cooking metaphor, we have an abundance of useful information about certain pots and pans that may be helpful in preparing a given dish. However, we know practically nothing about the ingredients, cooking techniques, or recipes that make the dish either detestable, palatable, or delicious. We also know very little about the training of the chefs and whether their specialties are with other forms of regional cuisine. The extent to which a dish is delicious is also very dependent on individual preferences. Ergo, understanding the target population's backgrounds and preferences is equally vital for successful presentation and implementation.

The Limitations of Methodological Individualism and Structuralism

If one accepts that success in college writing is dependent on a student's acclimation to the conventions of academic discourse, the following question becomes significant: *How* do students become acclimated to academic discourse communities that help them succeed in college writing coursework?

Traditionally, a sociologist asking this question might turn to one of two intellectual traditions: methodological individualism or structuralism (Kolluri & Tierney in this volume).[2] A viewpoint that embraces methodological individualism could answer that students—through human agency that encompasses sustained reading, critical inquiry, and emulating other writers well versed in the conventions of academic discourse—make a rational decision to devote time in service of developing their writing skills so they can produce "college-level" work. After those skills are developed, students can transform their newly acquired human capital into economic capital once they earn a college credential and find suitable employment (Tan 2014).

On the other hand, a viewpoint based on structuralism would hold that certain organizational components of a college education (e.g., the forms of academic support available, the instructors' capacity to work with students) are of paramount importance. These components regulate who gains access to vital information about writing that enables student achievement. Under a structuralist framework, the agency of the student is a less important determinant of academic success than the fluid transfer of knowledge from the institution to the student. To the extent a student has agency, it is dependent on intrinsic characteristics that enable them to grasp information quickly and comprehensively, thereby resulting in a discernible, positive effect on educational outcomes.

These two accounts of social reality represent credible, yet incomplete positions when considering the topic of college writing. In a first-year writing classroom, students undoubtedly have a certain degree of agency to affect outcomes. Nonetheless, their agency is constrained by previous educational and sociocultural experiences with writing and communication, the degree to which an instructor effectively conveys expectations for the course, the speed at which students can discern the instructor's priorities and adapt their writing styles to meet expectations, and a host of other considerations that potentially undermine positivistic investigation. At the same time, an overriding emphasis on social structure dictates, in perhaps an overdetermined manner, the types of writing-related opportunities available to students and the range of outcomes that can be achieved.

In short, a research study grounded in either methodological individualism or structuralism can only offer limited insights about the factors that curtail student achievement. Methodological individualism puts too much emphasis on student agency while neglecting the essential historical and sociocultural factors that influence student success. Meanwhile, structuralism is too fixated on organizational structure and the belief that if certain variables are tweaked appropriately, an ideal, generalizable set of conditions can be developed that facilitate nearly universal student development.

Most important, neither approach focuses on the essential condition under which students develop as writers: the relationships that enable them to understand the shared values and assumptions of a discourse community. Textbooks and workbook exercises can help students develop an understanding of specific grammatical and sentence-level expectations that enable basic communicative abilities in a given language. However, advanced writing skills in an educational institution are developed primarily through three relational activities: (1) the student's understanding of the instructor's stated guidelines and evaluative criteria for a writing assignment, (2) feedback on a piece of writing from established (and aspiring) members of a discourse community, and (3) revision of that writing to meet the explicated standards of that discourse community.

A Relational Framework for Understanding Writing

Similar to Kolluri and Tierney (in this volume), I am less interested in outlining a single procedure for relational research than in demonstrating a potentially fruitful way a researcher could grapple with a rich, multifaceted topic like college writing. With this caveat, I propose that these relationships can be better understood with three concepts that Desmond (2014) and Emirbayer (1997) associate with a relational framework: (1) transactions, (2) an examination of cultural conflict and power dynamics, and (3) an incorporation of the comprehensive field of study. The nature of the approach I suggest is also informed by Desmond's (2014) conceptualization of relational sociology, which involves studying "at least two types of actors or agencies occupying different positions within the social space and bound together in a relationship of mutual dependence or struggle" (554). As a result, the researcher is less concerned with "groups" or "places," as one might be in positivistic research that attempts to control variables—or even in a traditional ethnography that endeavors to understand and describe specific group behaviors through shared experience. Instead, the researcher focuses on the connections that bind actors together, the influence actors have on each other, and the networks constructed through these relationships.

Transactions

An initial step in unpacking these connections and networks is to consider the writing-related activities of paper development, feedback, and revision in a transactional way. Instead of analyzing the individual cognitive processes that create a piece of writing, a transactional approach might focus on student networks and the mutual exchange of information, guidance, and ideas that give shape to their writing. As described by Emirbayer (1997), such an approach means that the "dynamic, unfolding process" is "the primary unit of analysis" (287).

Hence, in an implicit rebuke of structuralism, the researcher focuses attention on processes rather than processed people (Desmond 2014). For a study of remedial writing, a researcher would be interested in the processes that affect student development in an effort to better understand the socially constructed factors that affect their completion of coursework. To give a simple example: when students confer with an instructor to find out if their resources are appropriate for citation, a transaction is taking place that contributes to the development of their critical and discriminatory skills. A researcher focused on transactions and processes might also detail the networks students rely on to make sense of course requirements, assignments, and instructor feedback. I explore this latter aspect of transactions in the first field narrative.

Cultural Conflict and Power Dynamics

A second implication resulting from a perspective informed by relational sociology is that a researcher studies cultural conflict in lieu of an emphasis on group culture. Desmond has stated that "the goal" of *Evicted* "was to study urban poverty without taking the urban poor or a poor community as [his] basic object of analysis" (2016, 563). Similarly, one might undertake a study of remedial writing without making students or a student community the singular focus of the investigation. Rather than viewing the individuals involved with remedial writing as being indicative of a solitary, homogeneous culture, one could think of the environment surrounding college writing classes as embodying "bundles of communications, relations, and transactions" (Emirbayer 1997, 300). Through such a prism, these bundles become valuable data for understanding the difficulties faced by students in college writing.

By perceiving the college writing classroom as a zone of cultural conflict, one can document and analyze power dynamics that may play a vital role in student outcomes. Even though sociocultural theory implies that writing is a shared group experience, much writing in educational settings is a private exchange between professor and student—or between student and tutor in a writing center. The relationships between professor and student, writing tutor and student, and professor and writing tutor are laden with power dynamics defined by field-specific norms (Bourdieu 1986). Depending on the organizational culture, some institutions may have less equitable distributions of power than others. Nevertheless, students are acutely aware that the writing they produce in college must please an audience of one—the professor—if they are to progress through their coursework. One should not presume that these interactions are always benign.

Therefore, researchers interested in investigating college writing would do well to consider the unspoken institutional expectations concerning authority and power. The racialized and gendered aspects of relationships that affect how students write—and the way professors grade—are also ripe for interrogation. The second field narrative offers an example of this form of cultural conflict.

The Comprehensive Field of Study

A third implication of the proposed framework involves the field of study. In a project that uses relational sociology, the researcher considers the comprehensive field of study, rather than a single site. A great deal of contemporary research on writing takes place entirely in a classroom or a writing center. Yet pertinent experiences that shape student perspectives on communication, as well as student views on writing, occur in numerous spaces inside and outside the college. Community-based discourse, for example, would require a more focused theoretical lens on the greater cultural and societal factors that affect the environment in which a college is embedded. Furthermore, relational studies of remediation would benefit from the documentation of broader interactions that occur in both physical space (e.g., beyond the college campus) and virtual space (e.g., through discussion boards and emails).

By expanding the boundaries of the field to the limits of social connections, rather than specific locations, a fuller picture of a research study's participants can be painted. Because of the relationships students cultivate during college, individual identities often evolve in interesting and unexpected ways. A relational framework allows for thick description that can depict these changes, instead of treating participants as static entities. The way students are compelled to alter their writing styles and expectations from institution to institution—or from classroom to classroom—can be accommodated by a relational framework. The third narrative provides an example of how students are compelled to radically change their writing-related expectations from high school to college.

A Few Words on Methodology

The Setting

To illustrate how transactions, cultural conflict, and a comprehensive field of study can be used as a framework for a relational sociology that investigates writing, I have selected three short narratives from a year-long ethnographic study of first-year writing at a four-year state college in Florida. The institution under study, referred to in this document by the pseudonym "Orange State College," annually serves between approximately 25,000 students (at the peak of the 2008 recession) to 18,000 students (in more recent years) on six campuses, offering more than 100 undergraduate degrees and certificates. It is by far the largest higher education institution within a metropolitan area of approximately 500,000 people.

Statistics indicate that approximately seven out of every ten students at Orange State live at or below the poverty threshold. According to data from the fall 2017 semester, only 39 percent of Orange State's students were able to attend classes on a full-time basis. The average age among students is twenty-seven; hence, few students enroll at Orange State immediately after graduating from high school. Instead, most arrive at Orange State after attending high schools in other regions of the United States, completing secondary education in other countries, or earning a GED after being away from school for several years.

To provide support for students in need of remediation, Orange State College developed one-hour "writing studios" that could be taken as corequisite coursework alongside first-year writing classes. The writing studios met once a week and usually enrolled four to twelve students. Writing studio "facilitators" (usually full-time tutors from the college writing center) organized peer review of papers, group feedback on a single paper or assignment, or supplemental lessons on specific writing-related topics, such as thesis statements, citations, or rhetorical analyses. These writing studios became a focal point for my study, as they facilitated access to students and provided a unique perspective on college writing.

How Theory Informed Methodology

I did not begin the Orange State ethnography with a relational framework in mind. After the first couple of weeks in the field, however, I became acutely aware of how significant the emerging bonds between students and studio facilitators were for retention. A distressingly large percentage of students received poor marks on their initial writing assignments, and the facilitators filled a role that was at once supportive and strategic. Students would regularly leave the writing studio with a plan of action for future assignments, feeling more confident about their potential to succeed by the end of the semester. The exploration of this fundamentally important relationship led me to consider other relationships, such as the developing bonds between groups of students, the manifold types of relationships between professors and students, and the less visible (but equally vital) relationships between faculty and staff, some of which were enacted exclusively through email or informal conversations.

Over the course of the ethnographic study, I conducted a total of ninety semi-structured interviews. These included twenty-two interviews with eleven writing tutors, thirty-eight student interviews, twelve interviews with administrators and academic support staff, thirteen interviews with instructors from first-year writing classes, and five interviews with high school English teachers. Because of my relational turn, the interview protocols evolved to include questions about interpersonal communications, feelings of marginalization that were engendered by feedback on assignments and classroom interactions, and students' writing experiences beyond Orange State College. In addition, I conducted twenty-one focus groups in writing studios and first-year writing classes that involved a total of 183 students. I logged approximately 150 hours of observations of tutoring sessions, writing studios, and first-year writing classes. The following narratives, intended to illustrate how relational sociology can focus attention on issues heretofore overlooked by research on remedial education, have been selected from this rich data set.

Three Narratives from a Relational Study of Remedial Writing

Transactions

THE NARRATIVE

Kristi is a thirty-five-year-old woman who confided that she was "initially nervous" in the writing studio. Even though she only had seven classmates in her studio, Kristi told me that it took "four to five weeks" before she really felt free "to speak up." At times, she would repeat phrases in the studio when she was anxious. Belying her outward appearance, however, was an exceptional determination to complete her associate's degree. Kristi has a learning disability that makes online and hybrid classes problematic. When advisors signed her up for online classes against her will at the beginning of the fall semester, she sent the head of the advising department an email and copied several high-ranking members of the college administration. Within minutes, a new advising meeting had been scheduled for her.

One day in the studio classroom, Gabe, the facilitator, asked each student about their upcoming writing assignments. When he approached Kristi, she laughed nervously and cried out, "I don't know what I'm doing! I don't know!" Gabe probed further, smiling as he approached:

> GABE: I don't believe that. What is your next assignment?
>
> KRISTI: A process—hold on—a process analysis. Yeah, that's it.
>
> GABE: Oh, I remember this assignment. Did he give you an example?
>
> KRISTI: Yes. It's called "Texas chili." We also have an explanation. Want to see?
>
> GABE: Sure. Let me come over there.

Gabe read the professor's explanation of a process analysis aloud to the class:

> Process analysis essays are directions. They explain how to do something, how something works, or how something happens. These essays present the steps in the process in chronological order, from first to last.
>
> GABE: Okay—first thing. Forget the term "process analysis" for a moment. This is really a "how to" paper. Does that make sense?
>
> KRISTI: A little. But I still don't know what I'll write about. You know that I get thoughts jumbled in my mind.

For the next twenty minutes, Gabe worked with the students who had to write a process analysis. I had to miss his next weekly studio because of an out-of-town conference. When I returned two weeks later, though, Kristi was beaming from ear to ear.

"I just got an 'A' on my 'how to!' " Turning to her friend, Kristi asked, "What was the technical word for it? What we just did?"

"A process analysis."

Kristi continued, enthusiastically, "I couldn't get it at all. I tried writing about changing a tire, but I kept getting stuck on the first steps. So, I had to change my way of thinking, because it was like a block. And Gabe helped me. He was like, 'What would you really do? It doesn't have to be true.' "

"So I made up a story of how to rob a bank." With this statement, Kristi got very excited, and her voice accelerated. "I don't know how to really rob a bank. I have no idea what's successful. . . . But, I can tell you what my essay's about!" At this point, Gabe and the other students smiled. Kristi continued:

> My essay starts off as, "Some people say to use a gun, but it's traceable. Some people say to a buy a car in cash, but it will break down on you. Some people say to lay low, or not to spend the money, but who wants to do that? So, let me tell you what I would use: a donkey, a mirror, and a Zorro mustache." Those were things I picked—those were the topics of my sentences.
>
> I realized that the donkey can put stuff in his hind compartment, which is under his tail. And then I think about, "Well, what am I going to do with the donkey when I'm done?" Well, I put him on a farm, and I work him on the farm. Then I sell him. Extra money!
>
> So I now use the mirror. I stand in front of the mirror and say, "You look good! I can do this! I am going to be successful today!"
>
> Finally, the Zorro mustache makes people think I'm crazy. No one is going to be fooled by it. But they might be worried about what I might do, if they try to stop me.
>
> I'm able to stay on topic. I'm able to do what my teacher wanted. But I'm also able to be creative—open to do whatever I want to do—but stay inside the rules!

Kristi realized that she was fortunate that her teacher appreciated how her imagination sparked her ability to write. "My teacher could have said 'no.' And I don't know what I would've done."

DISCUSSION AND ANALYSIS

The first important transaction in this narrative is between Kristi and her studio facilitator, Gabe. Kristi might have never started her process analysis essay if Gabe had not reenvisioned the prompt in a way that sparked her creativity and imagination. Moreover, by encouraging her to visualize an absurd, yet humorous scenario, Gabe helped Kristi meet the essential demands of the assignment—to explain a process in step-by-step detail—without being stifled by emotional factors, such as boredom or a lack of confidence.

The second important transaction in this narrative occurred outside of the classroom. Due to the unconventional way she approached the assignment, it is quite possible that other professors would have told Kristi that her essay was not a proper process analysis. Gabe, however, knew Kristi's professor and consulted with him before she committed a single word to the page. The professor, cognizant of Kristi's challenges, okayed the topic. The professor later shared with me that he "was delighted that [Kristi] was excited about a writing assignment. It might have been the only one."

Such a relationship between studio facilitators and writing instructors was not terribly common at Orange State. However, Gabe worked at a branch campus where individuals from different levels of the university regularly engaged in conversation outside of the classroom. An organizational theorist might expand on such an analysis by arguing that Gabe's connection to the faculty, facilitated by a flattened institutional structure and a relatively circumscribed setting, allowed for a transaction of information about Kristi and her intentions for the writing assignment—all of which worked to her benefit.

Cultural Conflict and Power Dynamics

THE NARRATIVE

Mikayla, a White female writing studio facilitator, worked as an English instructor and tutor at multiple research universities in the Northeast

United States before landing at Orange State. Two Black female students in her studio, Felicia and Dawn, were doing well in their nonwriting coursework, but they were irritated by their White male writing instructor. Toward the end of the fall semester, they shared details about their first-year writing class with Mikayla.

> MIKAYLA: Do you know when you'll find out your grade?
>
> DAWN: I'll find out on Friday when [my professor] grades our papers in class.
>
> MIKAYLA: That's when he gives the papers back to people, or . . . ?
>
> DAWN: He'll look at [the papers], and he'll tell you exactly what you did wrong. But then I'll be looking at him like "You didn't tell me or give me more information to help me be a better writer."
>
> MIKAYLA: Wait. So you just give the papers back [to him], and he grades it right there for you?
>
> FELICIA: That's why I wait until the end of class to give my paper to him.
>
> [Several people in the studio laughed.]
>
> MIKAYLA: Does he write feedback on your paper?
>
> DAWN: No! It's like "awkward" or "slang." But you're not telling me what's "awkward" and what is "slang!"
>
> FELICIA: How do I know what's slang? I said "fun," and he said it was slang.
>
> Mikayla audibly groaned in sympathy. Then, she asked another question, "How is the rest of the class doing?"

Dawn: The older students are just saying, "If I don't get it done now, I'll never get it done." So they spend a lot of time outside of class looking for help.

Felicia: Yeah, the younger students seem to have stopped coming to class.

Mikayla: Out of curiosity, how many students are in your class?

Dawn: Hmm—twenty-five?

Mikayla: So that would be a lot of conferences.

Dawn: But that's what we had at the beginning. We're probably down to ten.

Mikayla: Seriously?

Dawn: Yes. The other day, we were literally down to six people in class.

Mikayla: Oh my God.

DISCUSSION AND ANALYSIS

This narrative raises numerous questions about power dynamics, racially charged language, and student attrition. Dawn and Felicia, along with the other students in the writing class, experienced a performative representation of their instructor's power over their grades, as they were compelled to physically bring their written work to him during class for assessment. Hence, it is unsurprising that their relationship with the instructor was quite distant, and they were routinely perplexed by his expectations and grading procedures. Compounding the issue, the professor seemed to be fixated on enumerating errors, rather than explaining how students might revise their work to meet the demands of the assignment. If college writing is a conceptual field, as Bourdieu (1986) might suggest, such apparent power imbalances limit the ability of students to learn from their mistakes. Even worse, their experiences with such an instructor might shape their habitus in ways that could negatively affect their views of instructor–student interactions and their performance in future college coursework.

The power dynamics at Orange State were such that a studio facilitator, like Mikayla, had limited agency to intervene on behalf of students like Dawn and Felicia, other than to provide emotional support and develop strategies for future paper revisions. The fact that Mikayla, despite her experience, was a relatively new female hire at Orange State, and the White male writing professor in question had been entrenched in the college for over twenty-five years, was also an issue potentially loaded with power dynamics. Unlike Gabe in the previous narrative, Mikayla did not have a proximal organizational climate that encouraged feedback or shared information between faculty and staff. Thus, the potential for auspicious transactions between facilitator and professor—or even student and professor—were fractured by cultural conflict.

A researcher employing critical race theory might analyze the foregoing narrative and find that other instructors at Orange State use similar racially charged language as "slang" to critique papers by Black or Hispanic students. It is also possible that the writing instructors at Orange State College, the vast majority of whom are White and middle- to upper-class, are unaware of their biases in assessing the work of students from different international, multicultural, or socioeconomic backgrounds. In one interview, a White instructor who originally earned a graduate degree in rhetoric and composition from a prominent university was candid about this issue. She detailed how her stance on first-year writing gradually evolved, after several years of teaching at Orange State.

> I think when I first started at [Orange State] I was still pretty rigid about getting students to sound like an academic writer. But, as I started to think about it, there have been very few situations where I have legitimately been unable to understand somebody's message because of simple grammar errors. It's just that we want them to write like us, and we write like middle-class White people and, probably even hyper-academic, middle-class White people, and that's not who our students are.
>
> Ten years ago, I would not have said that my classroom was political, but now I believe it absolutely is. The composition classroom is always political.

Issues surrounding race, ethnicity, and class are often glossed over in the outcome-oriented quantitative research on remediation, but they are worthy of greater attention because they can have a robust impact on student retention and completion rates. As Dawn and Felicia state, the younger students stopped attending class to avoid dealing with the professor's dismissive attitude and lack of interest in giving information that could help them become better writers. Similar cultural and class-related disparities between college instructors and their students are deserving of further investigation for substantive progress on writing outcomes.

Comprehensive Field of Study

THE NARRATIVE

At the end of the fall semester, two recent high school graduates in a focus group declared that they were "tired of their classmates complaining":

> STUDENT 1: If [teachers] give you a time to put it in, to have it corrected, to submit it. You do it. You don't ask questions.
>
> STUDENT 2: It's not high school. You know—in high school, sometimes, that would work. You could turn in your paper a few days late.
>
> STUDENT 1: You could turn in your paper a *month* late.
>
> MICHAEL: So were your experiences in high school like that? You could turn in work late?
>
> <Everyone in unison>: Yes!

Writing instructors at Orange State who previously worked in a Florida high school verified the students' perceptions of high school deadlines. Therefore, I expanded my field of study to interview five teachers who worked at public high schools near Orange State College. Two shared the following details about deadlines and grades in their high school classes:

> HS TEACHER 1: This is not how I would like to work, but students can turn in assignments the very last day of school, and I have to take them. And I have to grade them. I know one teacher who called it "extra credit."
>
> HS TEACHER 2: Also, I know one school where if students turn in stuff and then fail, [they can] take an optional test

and still pass the whole class. So I think a lot of [students] did that.

MICHAEL: So that explains why I've heard some students say that they didn't actually write [a paper] during their last two years of high school.

HS TEACHER 2: Right.

One writing professor at Orange State was acutely aware of these practices because her spouse was still teaching in the high school system. When she first started teaching at Orange State, she encouraged students to turn in an extra paper at the end of the semester for extra credit. However, that activity quickly got out of hand:

INSTRUCTOR: Before I knew what was going on, I had students coming up to me all the time, asking, "Oh, what else can I do?" "Do I have to turn this paper in if I give you a different paper?" It was madness.

MICHAEL: What caused that?

INSTRUCTOR: [The students] believe that's what you do to get an A. My spouse actually laughs at my syllabus. He says it would last one week in his school.

MICHAEL: So, they think that's the norm for coursework?

INSTRUCTOR: Exactly. Right. In a way, they've been trained to actually negotiate like that.

In a different focus group in the spring, several students shared their "shock" at the strict deadlines demanded by their professors. One commentary from a woman in her mid-twenties named Tiffany received scattered applause from her fellow students: "I have a child at home. I have an old car that sometimes dies, and you know that public transportation to this campus is a joke. I have a lot of time management skills, but I don't really have *time* when I have to be with my kids, my family, and go to my job. So some of these instructors need to know that—it's hard."

DISCUSSION AND ANALYSIS

The issue of deadlines exemplifies how noncognitive factors, as much as cognitive factors, can function as a determinant of student success in first-year writing. In high school, a student's relationship with a teacher could lead to protracted deadlines or even a completely different assignment. However, one finding from Orange State College was that the ability of a student to meet deadlines in an environment unforgiving to late work and less conducive to communication was as effective as a student's writing skills. In short, the ability to complete a writing assignment on time was a primary determinant of a student's "college readiness."

College professors and students in remediation were quick to blame high school culture for students' lack of urgency concerning deadlines, as multiple people stated that a culture of "social promotion" had acculturated students into thinking that deadlines and grades were negotiable. Expanding the field of study to include high school teachers verified some of these claims. The objective social conditions of local public high schools shaped student dispositions toward writing in profound ways that were detrimental to their performance in college writing classes.

An expansion of the temporal parameters of research, however, allowed me to conduct more focus groups that revealed more complex realities congruent with Tiffany's assertion: "I have a lot of time management skills, but I don't really have *time* when I have to be with my kids, my family, and go to my job." Even while working one or more jobs, students at Orange State were often financially on the edge. An unexpected medical bill, an obligatory car repair, a late payment from financial aid, or other unforeseen factors could cause a student to miss class, turn in work late, or prioritize their work and family responsibilities over their education.

Many professors were sympathetic to these student realities, but they were also under exceptional pressure because of heavy course loads, and they had little time to develop relationships outside of the classroom. A sociologist operating from a Marxist view of labor, capitalism, and exploitation (e.g., Wright 2000) might note that full-time instructors at Orange State carry a five-five teaching load in the fall and spring semesters, with additional class assignments every summer. Writing classes have no fewer than twenty students. A more common course load is twenty-five to thirty students. Since writing instructors at Orange State are expected to assign four to five papers per class, they provide feedback to at least 500 papers in a single semester. If an instructor allows students to revise their papers for a higher grade, the number of papers receiving feedback could approach 1,000. Under such conditions, it is understandable that instructors kept strict timelines so they could provide useful feedback, give students time to revise their work, and move the class forward to the next institutionally mandated writing assignment.

Conclusion

This chapter serves as a starting point for deeper consideration of how research on college remediation, particularly with regard to writing, might be conducted using a relational sociology framework. Although much current work on remediation has focused on outcomes, there is a need for expanded methodological approaches and a deeper integration with theory. I have asserted that future research could benefit from prolonged engagement in the field that investigates and analyzes the relationships forged between students, high school teachers, college instructors, and other important institutional actors. The three narratives presented in this chapter depict how relational sociology can (1) examine the transactional nature of writing, (2) shed light on the inevitable cultural conflicts and power dynamics in an institutional setting, and (3) expand the field of study to embrace multiple relevant perspectives—all in service of a deeper, more inclusive understanding of the factors that affect student success.

This relational framework is not intended to be comprehensive. Instead, I hope that this chapter will inspire other researchers to conceptualize frameworks that focus on relationships, rather than circumscribed categories or static individual characteristics. In doing so, we can move beyond what works to a more compelling explanation of why and how certain educational approaches work, under what conditions, and through which relationships.

Notes

1. Remedial education—also known as "developmental education" or "basic skills education"—refers to a segment of the US higher education sector that equips underprepared students with the skills necessary for college-level coursework.

2. The term "holism" has also been used in place of "structuralism," most notably by Charles Tilly (2002).

References

Attewell, P., Lavin, D., Domina, T., & Levey, T. (2006). New evidence on college remediation. *Journal of Higher Education*, *77*(5), 886–924.

Bailey, T., Jaggars, S. S., & Scott-Clayton, J. (2013). *Characterizing the effectiveness of developmental education: A response to recent criticism*. New York, NY: Community College Research Center, Teachers College, Columbia University.

Belfield, C., Jenkins, D., & Lahr, H. (2016). *Is corequisite remediation cost-effective? Early findings from Tennessee* (CCRC Research Brief No. 62). New York, NY: Community College Research Center, Teachers College, Columbia University.

Boatman, A. R. (2012). *Evaluating institutional efforts to streamline postsecondary remediation*. PhD diss., Harvard University.

Boatman, A. R., & Long, B. T. (2018). Does remediation work for all students? How the effects of postsecondary remediation and developmental courses vary by level of academic preparation. *Educational Evaluation and Policy Analysis*, *40*(1), 29–58.

Bourdieu, P. (1986). The forms of capital. In *Handbook of theory and research for the sociology of education*, edited by J. G. Richardson, 241–58. New York, NY: Greenwood Press.

Callahan, R. M. (2005). Tracking and high school English learners: Limiting opportunity to learn. *American Educational Research Journal*, *42*(2), 305–28.

Clotfelter, C. T., Ladd, H. F., Muschkin, C., & Vigdor, J. L. (2015). Developmental education in North Carolina community colleges. *Educational Evaluation and Policy Analysis*, *37*(3), 354–75.

Complete College America. (2012). *Remediation: Higher education's bridge to nowhere*. Washington, DC: Complete College America. Retrieved from http://completecollege.org/docs/CCA-Remediation-final.pdf.

Desmond, M. (2014). Relational ethnography. *Theory and Society*, *43*(5), 547–79.

Desmond, M. (2016). *Evicted: Poverty and profit in the American city*. New York, NY: Crown.

Emirbayer, M. (1997). Manifesto for a relational sociology. *American Journal of Sociology*, *103*(2), 281–317.

Frey, C. B., & Osborne, M. A. (2017). The future of employment: How susceptible are jobs to computerization? *Technological Forecasting and Social Change*, *114*, 254–80.

Gee, J. P. (2015). *Social linguistics and literacies: Ideology in discourses* (5th ed.). London, UK: Routledge.

Hodara, M., & Xu, D. (2016). Does developmental education improve labor market outcomes? Evidence from two states. *American Educational Research Journal*, *53*(3), 781–813.

Jaggars, S. S., Hodara, M., Cho, S. W., & Xu, D. (2015). Three accelerated developmental education programs: Features, student outcomes, and implications. *Community College Review*, *43*(1), 3–26.

Jimenez, L., Sargrad, S., Morales, J., & Thompson, M. (2016). *Remedial education: The cost of catching up*. Center for American Progress. Retrieved from https://www.americanprogress.org/issues/education-k-12/reports/2016/09/28/144000/remedial-education/

Lanford, M. (2019). Making sense of "outsiderness": How life history informs the college experiences of "nontraditional" students. *Qualitative Inquiry, 25*(5), 500–512.

Levin, H. M., & Calcagno, J. C. (2008). Remediation in the community college: An evaluator's perspective. *Community College Review, 35*(3), 181–207.

Logue, A. W., Watanabe-Rose, M., & Douglas, D. (2016). Should students assessed as needing remedial mathematics take college-level quantitative courses instead? A randomized controlled trial. *Educational Evaluation and Policy Analysis, 38*(3), 578–98.

Lumina Foundation. (2014). *A stronger nation through higher education*. Indianapolis, IN: Lumina Foundation.

National Student Clearinghouse Research Center. (2017). *Snapshot report—first-year persistence and retention*. Retrieved from https://nscresearchcenter.org/wp-content/uploads/SnapshotReport28a.pdf

Oakes, J., & Guiton, G. (1995). Matchmaking: The dynamics of high school tracking decisions. *American Educational Research Journal, 32*(1), 3–33.

Prior, P. (2006). A sociocultural theory of writing. In *Handbook of writing research*, edited by C. A. MacArthur, S. Graham, & J. Fitzgerald, 54–66). New York, NY: Guilford Press.

Scott-Clayton, J., Crosta, P. M., & Belfield, C. R. (2012). *Improving the targeting of treatment: Evidence from college remediation* (NBER Working Paper no. 18457). Cambridge, MA: National Bureau of Economic Research.

Tan, E. (2014). Human capital theory: A holistic criticism. *Review of Educational Research, 84*(3), 411–45.

Tilly, C. (2002). *Stories, identities, and political change*. Lanham, MD: Rowman & Littlefield.

US Census Bureau. (2017). *Education attainment in the United States: 2016*. Retrieved from https://www.census.gov/data/tables/2016/demo/education-attainment/cps-detailed-tables.html

Vygotsky, L. S. (1934/1986). *Thought and language*, edited by A. Kozulin. Boston, MA: MIT Press.

Wright, E. O. (2000). Class, exploitation, and economic rents: Reflections on Sorenson's "sounder basis." *American Journal of Sociology, 105*(6), 1559–71.

Contributors

William G. Tierney is university professor, Wilbur-Kieffer Professor of Higher Education, and co-director of the Pullias Center for Higher Education at the University of Southern California. He is the past president of the American Educational Research Association (AERA) and the Association for the Study of Higher Education. He is an AERA Fellow and a member of the National Academy of Education.

Suneal Kolluri is a postdoctoral scholar at the University of California, Riverside. He is a National Board–certified teacher who earned his PhD from the University of Southern California. He taught for nine years in Oakland public schools. His research focuses on how secondary schools can improve college access and persistence for underrepresented youth.

anthony lising antonio is associate director of the Stanford Institute for Higher Education Research and associate professor of education at Stanford University. His research focuses on stratification and postsecondary access, racial diversity and its impact on students and institutions, student friendship networks, and student development.

Joseph J. Ferrare is assistant professor in the Department of Educational Policy Studies and Evaluation at the University of Kentucky, where he also holds appointments in the Department of Sociology and Martin School of Public Policy. His research focuses broadly on understanding how social inequalities are created within the education system and the policies and practices that can ameliorate these inequalities to facilitate upward social mobility.

Jesse Foster is a lead researcher and project manager with Evaluation and Assessment Solutions for Education. She earned her doctorate in sociology of education from Stanford University. Her research focuses on the experiences of first-generation college students in high schools that are working to improve their college-going cultures.

Tamara Gilkes Borr is a doctoral candidate in the sociology of education program at the Graduate School of Education at Stanford University. She is a recipient of the Institute of Education Sciences fellowship, the National Academy of Education/Spencer fellowship (declined), and Stanford University's Diversifying Academia Recruiting Excellence fellowship.

Hoori S. Kalamkarian is postdoctoral research associate with the Community College Research Center at Teachers College, Columbia University. Kalamkarian holds a BA in English and political science from University of California, Los Angeles, and a PhD in education policy from Stanford University.

Michael Lanford is a postdoctoral scholar at the Pullias Center for Higher Education at the University of Southern California. Before earning his doctorate, he worked as a writing center administrator and college humanities instructor. His research explores innovative approaches to secondary and higher education, focusing on student development, educational policy, and the impact of globalization.

Janice McCabe is associate professor of sociology and the Allen House Professor at Dartmouth College. Her book, *Connecting in College: How Friendship Networks Matter for Academic and Social Success* (2016), and current research focus on friendship networks and identities during college and into young adulthood. She is interested in how gender, race/ethnicity, and social class operate as social identities and how they shape social networks.

Julie R. Posselt is assistant professor of higher education at the University of Southern California. Rooted in sociological and organizational theory, Posselt's research examines institutionalized inequalities in higher education, especially in selective sectors such as graduate education and STEM disciplines. She is author of the book *Inside Graduate Admissions: Merit,*

Diversity, and Faculty Gatekeeping, and is currently coleading three National Science Foundation–funded studies examining equity and inclusion in STEM graduate education.

Antar A. Tichavakunda is assistant professor in the School of Education at the University of Cincinnati. He earned his PhD in urban education policy from the University of Southern California. Prior to his studies, Tichavakunda taught high school English in Washington, DC, public schools. His research focuses on increasing college access, Black students' experiences at predominantly White institutions, and the sociology of higher education.

Index

Page numbers in *italics* refer to figures and tables.

www.ingramcontent.com/pod-product-compliance
Lightning Source LLC
LaVergne TN
LVHW050153080826
844660LV00002B/189